With this book, the knowledge limits of higher dimension only one thought beyond us have been overcome, the mental lock of the visible world has been unlocked and the awaited transition has begun!

**Welcome to The Golden of Knowledge
Of the Dimension Where Time and Space
DO NOT EXIST...**

The Golden of Knowledge

Research-Observing: 2

•

Page Design : Exit Typography Unit

•

Cover Design : Aydın TÜRKGÜCÜ , Soner ÖZLÜ

•

Translation : Özge ESİRGEN

•

Printing History

January 2015, İstanbul, Turkey - Printing House: Sena

ISBN 978-975-6861-06-6

•

www.aydinturkgucu.net

CONTENTS

Thank You

They asked a dervish, "What is the wisdom of a dervish?"
The Dervish answered, "To be patient when he has nothing,
To give thanks when he has something."
You spoke well brother dervish, but the important thing is this:
"To be patient when you have nothing,
And to be able to share when you have something."

There are two types of writers, the active writer and the passive writer. Those who write books are active writers, those who have a part in writing the book, knowingly or not, are the passive writers.

First and foremost to my family and to those who have shared their knowledge and experience, to all I have had the opportunity to know and to those I haven't met, and to those who have contributed to this book intentionally or unknowingly, I extend my heartfelt gratitude.

My only claim is my sincerity.

Aydın TÜRKGÜCÜ

Thinker & Thought-Stimulator

Stepping Out Of Darkness Into the Light, The Last Step Will Come From Us

FOREWORD

One of the several ways to end the wars and fighting is to deprciate what's fought for. I prepared this book, which is based on a scientific basis and scientific data as far as possible;

- To have a contact with you

- Receive the first **'Nobel Peace Prize'** which serves not only the peace amongst humans but peace amongst every being in the universe whether animate or inanimate

- And of course for 'Him'.

We are living in a universe where even a minor detail can create a crucial level of awareness or an ordinary thought can change everything. Please contribute with your ideas, share your thoughts even if it's about a very small detail, if you are one of those who think they would write, tell, express something differently than I did. Be one of those who write this book for the new edition.

The personal successes and failures as well as the happiness and the unhappiness that we experienced have helped us specialize in different areas of the whole. While moving to a phase of social development from a phase of personal development and reckoning what hasn't manifested yet, let us be amongst those who write, explain and design the future with the new answers and questions we will find. Let us be one of those who think and stimulate others to think.

One has to start by questioning the time and space he is living in, if he is to understand that he is in a dream…

"The Golden Age of KNOWLEDGE" and Holistic Peace

One can only achieve to end something if he destroys its philosophy. One way to avoid and put an end fighting and wars on a holistic scale is devaluing the means that we fight for.

Through the advancement in science and technology which brings forward new life forms in which our known notions of time and space undergo a transformation, our approach to humans, nature and universe change forever. This new approach revealed through the disciplines of Virtual Reality, Holographic Universe and Quantum Thought serves for a permanent holistic peace as it changes our views on war and peace, and especially the material and moral values that are fought for.

It is told that there is a Golden Age when everyone is happy and peaceful and there are no wars while the Holistic Peace is experienced based on material abundance.

<u>There are two ways for the wars to come to an end so that the permanent peace can reside;</u>

Abundance: We usually make wars for the sake of a better life to obtain forcibly what we don't have. No one would be fighting with others for more if everyone has it abundantly. It is obligatory for the Golden Age in which abundance, plentifulness, love and respect rule over everything else, that anything such as oil, water, gold, precious metals etc. that are fought for are abundant enough to satisfy everyone.

Unfortunately, it seems that the choice of Golden Age which is also described as 'heaven on earth' is not likely to take place in the near future considering that the depleting resources of energy and sustenance will have to be divided amongst more people. 'No one would be fighting for gold if gold was found as abundantly as the iron' yet mankind would find another rare mineral and fight for the sake of it. (it is predicted that there will be wars because of water, which is the most abundant thing found in our planet.)

Both Abundance and Scarcity: Another way of avoiding and ending the fights and wars in a holistic way is to ensure that everything that we fight for is indispensable for life while they also become too insignificant to cause wars between people. Summarizing it with the quantum thought; everything that is fought over should both subsist and perish at the same time.

You pay attention and adopt the realm of illusionary time and space you experience in your dreams unless you understand that they are dreams. When you recognize that you are in a dream, everything including the people, the places and the things you fight for lose their value and meaning. The definitions used for the worldly life follow as *'Realm of Fancies'*, *' Dream'*, *'Illusion'* or *'Delusion'*. What they all try to remind us is 'None of the things you see and value in life is real, whether animate or inanimate, they are all illusions. None of them is valuable enough to cause you to kill people, animals and the nature.'

The awakening from the dream in this worldly life can be in two ways as being **From Without** and **From Within**:

> **(1) From Without:** It awakens you from without by urging and shaking you. This type of awakening is realized by making the dream collapse through a physical impact such as volcanic eruptions, earthquakes or meteor hits which are described as the signs of apocalypse. Yet this is a FORCED AWAKENING rather than being a real awakening.
>
> **(2) From Within:** The AWAKENING that we seek as expected by everyone is awakening while we are still in the dream. But how are we going to awaken in a dream which derives its power from its unsolvableness?

They say *'The teacher appears when the student is ready'*. What I say is 'The answer appears when you ask the right question.' The first thing we should do to wake up from this worldly dream is to change the paradigm by asking 'What Are We Living In?' instead of the questions that start with 'Why and From Where'.

As a computer programmer, I have been trying to create awareness in my books, speeches and writings since 1995 by using the Ancient Knowledge and the concepts of the

Virtual Reality and Holographic Universe in the Holy Scriptures. I am working for the Holistic Peace which targets not only the peace between human beings but also the peace with one's self and later with every being, animate/inanimate, including the nature and the animals. I am much eager to spread the awareness and I give seminars called FUTURE WORKSHOPS for that purpose.

While giving new answers to the question 'What is it that we live in?', I also make people ask new questions in my book 'The Golden Age of Knowledge' which starts the Golden Age of KNOWLEDGE by making a fundamental change in the concept of the Traditional Universe. Through the designs of Virtual Reality and Holographic Universe that transform science-fiction into science,

1. I devalue the things that are fought over by helping people to direct their pursue of happiness from having material wealth to attaining the knowledge of the material realm. (The wars will prevail until the reality of matter collapses.)

2. I say '**Do not decide who created it and how to live in it before understanding what it is that you are living in!**' for the expected awakening from this worldly dream that we currently live in.

3. **I start an awareness through asking the questions 'Why Did God Create the Animals?' and 'Why Are There Animals?'**

4. **I suggest that the original Holy Grail is the human Brain.**

5. **And I say that the Golden Age of KNOWLEDGE can explain the Theory of Everything.**

Considering that the questions 'Where did we come from and Why did we come?' have been asked in way that **anyone can comprehend** since my second book (1998), the answer should be in a way that **anyone can find** as well. God would have been unfair to people on the streets if He had concealed it in a way only the scientists or the religious could find. I claim that **God has chosen His prophets generally from the ordinary people as if saying 'The Theory of Everything = The Theory of Everyone'**, in order to show the simplicity of the answer he concealed and encourage the ordinary people.

The stone age and the bronze age were ages when humans learnt how to rule over the matter while the first-middle-new and the modern age have been worldly ages when a power defeated another. The Golden Age of Knowledge is the first age that is not worldly and based on only knowledge. It is the age of transition which will take humanity to the GOLDEN AGE.

One way to serve for peace and provide peace is to support the efforts shown for the sake of peace. The over one-hundred-year history of the Peace Prize shows that there are many different paths to peace.

When I heard the question 'Who would be going to the battlefront if everyone knew the reality?' years ago, I realized that those who fight may not be fighting for the thing they think they are fighting. Shortly, what they were saying was 'They would not fight if they knew the reality and those who have been fighting would stop it.'

As the new life forms in which the known concepts of time and space are transformed are brought to agenda, we should support the recent viewpoints that can provide the holistic peace by changing our approach to humans, nature, animals and the universe forever. We have come to a point where we can show to those who fight what it is that they are really fighting for. Shortly, we have come to the point to see Holistic Peace realized throughout the world, which ever seemed quite impossible.

Through the re-interpretation of the will of Alfred Nobel by the Nobel Peace Committee with respect to the recent advancements, I believe that those who serve peace by creating awareness in the areas of Peace With Animals, Peace With Nature and Holistic Peace should be rewarded through the new categories.

With My Most Sincere Love and Respect

Aydın TÜRKGÜCÜ
Thinker & Thought-Stimulator
www.aydinturkgucu.net

DREAMMATIC

*Voice: Make a wish to **US,** whatever you wish. Say **LET THERE BE**, so that it is there at once!*

I opened my eyes the moment I heard these words. But it did not take me long to realize that there was no point in doing so, as there was nothing to see in the utter darkness. **The Voice** that said 'Are you ready?' in 2009, was saying **'Make a wish to US, whatever you wish!'** this time.

The best way to evaluate the credibility of such an offer is to try it. First, I should say 'Let there be light' to get out of this absolute darkness.

<u>Wish-1:</u> I said **'I want a luxurious beachfront mansion in a place where pine trees merge the sea on a beautiful summer morning.'** but nothing happened. Why doesn't it happen, is this a joke?

*Voice: It will happen when you say '**LET THERE BE**' at the beginning of each of your wishes.*

I repeated it right away, **'LET THERE BE a luxurious beachfront mansion full of luxury belonging to me, in a place where pine trees merge the sea on a beautiful summer morning.'**

As soon as I said this, I found myself gazing into a deep blue sea from the balcony of my mansion, just like I dreamt. You should have seen the splendid pine forest behind the house! It was the most beautiful forest you could ever see! I felt the wind that blew softly and that the beautiful landscape was good for my soul.

Glory be! I have reached the **Garden of Pleasures**, the abode of **Holy Retirement**, after completing the world test successfully. I was in my infinite buckshee abode whose limits and content would be defined by me; the abode where anything I wanted manifested plentifully. This should have been the way God gives His boons. Now that my initial wish has come true, I could continue on with them. I thought I should definitely ask for the houris[1] if I was in Heaven and decided to add a little sauciness to my wishes:

Wish-2: 'LET THERE BE a harem of different races that I own and a personnel that will serve us food and drinks we want and a yacht ready with its captain and crew right before my mansion.'

As I articulated it, I could not help feeling curious and excited upon hearing the voices of cheerful women coming from inside. Flashing with their enchanting smiles, four beautiful ladies approached me and began to behave quite

---

[1] The **houris** are translated as "(splendid) companions of equal age (well-matched)" "lovely eyed", of "modest gaze", "pure beings" or "companions pure" of paradise, denoting humans and jinn who enter Paradise after being recreated anew in the hereafter.

intimately. The personnel was preparing a splendid break-
fast. Just like it was told, anything I wished for was hap-
pening instantly beyond my expectations, the moment I
said **'LET THERE BE.'** This was exactly how patience in
a challenging worldly lifetime should be awarded afterwards. These women, whose touches and looks were created to bring down the limits of human willpower, were designed in a way that would imparadise any mortal being.

Just seconds before I was totally captured, caught by the
mesmerizing breeze of my houris, I realized that I did not
want to be a callow who chased after what he saw in a
place where I had the right to wish for anything I liked. I
decided to save myself from this first shock by hastily
wishing for something else. I was so eager to wish for
something new, excited like a child who has just found a
new toy, but then I thought that I should have to be careful
with what I wish in a place where anything I want happens
instantly. At the same time I supposed that such a high
technology couldn't have been produced just for property,
sexual fantasies and appetite.

*Voice: Why do you look down on the basic needs like food
or sex? How will you go on to the next holy stage without
them?*

**It felt quite uneasy to realize that my mind was being
read. What you are saying represents the ego and the
ego should be demolished.**

Voice: *Ego is the struggle between the body and the mind, each exchange (any kind of exchange whether material, emotional or spiritual) is a struggle that you have with your ego. The body depends on the laws of nature and it has necessities. Whereas in will power, there are possibilities, choices in other words. But the choices may oblige you to live a life you don't want to. In the words of Dr. Mehmet Öz: 'your body adapts to you so you can eat what you want. If you don't have proper nourishment and if you harm your body and get sick, then it turns out to be you who should adapt to your body and you start a diet.'*

Are they mistaken in saying 'get rid of your ego or defeat it'?

Voice: *When you consider the ego through the lens of your ego, you perceive this advice, which is getting rid of and chastening your ego as getting rid of the basic physical needs of the material world like food, drink or sex. It is not the ego that's bad; what's bad is being driven by the command of your ego and hindering others' lives and rights or harming yourself and others in the cause of your insatiable material/moral desires. In short, use your ego but do not get used to it, do not be attached to it.*

By saying 'Get rid of your ego' or 'defeat your ego', it is meant that 'you should evaluate your experiences and see if they are for the benefit of all or not, instead of pursuing the benefits it will bring to your body or your daily life.

Only then will you be able to see the hidden message in what's visible, the essence of the message in other words. Now, relax and just LET THERE BE whatever you want!

Let me wish for something, so that it will manifest, I thought. And I continued to design my own heaven.

<u>Wish-3</u>

LET THERE BE

- **A workplace in a villa with a terrace and a bosphorus view,**

- **A consulting company with an opinion and practice team producing ideas, technologies, solutions and projects for a better world,**

- **The title 'Thinker & Thought-Stimulator' written on my door and on my business card,**

- **A room for treasury the my company, full of cash money and gold bullion just like the lockbox of the Central Bank,**

- **They always talk about the rivers of milk in Heaven, let me wish and see if it happens. A river of milk, actually of goat milk, near my workplace.**

- **A sports car and even a helicopter as well,**

-    I always wanted to be an astronaut since my childhood. A spaceship in the garden, by which I can easily go to space and travel between the stars.

Upon my words, I was in the terrace of a superb villa with a bosphorus view, I startled by the rumble of a river of milk flowing splashing. My spaceship was waiting for me ready for launch in my back yard. The helicopter and the sports car were ready as well. Taking a look at the rooms quickly, I first found my co-workers and then my room of treasury which was wealthy enough to make even the sultans envy. Everything was just perfect.

(going out to terrace once again, looking at the starts)

'Aren't there any limits, prohibitions or rules?' I asked.

Voice: There is only one prohibition. You mustn't eat from the fruits of the QUINCE[2] tree that you will see in a corner every place you go; or you will be dismissed from this beautiful place which you could stay forever. By the way, you don't need to go outdoors or look above to talk to me. I hear and see you from wherever you are.

Forbidden tree, forbidden fruit… Am I dead, am I in Heaven?

---

[2] 'Eating the quince' is an idiom used in Turkish, which denotes that someone is in great trouble.

*Voice: We call this place **DREAMMATIC** where every-thing you wish for becomes a reality the moment as you dream of it.*

A world of dreams where all dreams come true: 'Fake Heaven'.

Voice: Think of it as a dream you wrote the scenario and designated the actors for and enjoy it just as if you are in heaven.

Can I unlimitedly wish for anything just like I am in heaven? Is this a dream? I should understand to keep going. Where am I? Am I dead?

Voice: Of course you aren't. You are just having experiences in another dimension's reality. There is no limit to wanting here. No insolence, no sin... More importantly, there is no fear of lacking or losing... When your wish comes true; you live in your dream until you want something new, and unless you eat QUINCE from the QUINCE tree. Allow your craziest dreams to take shape, do whatever you like, wish and LET THERE BE, and then, just enjoy...

Is it not a contradiction that you say 'do not eat the QUINCE' in a place where you claim that anything will just manifest once I say 'LET THERE BE'?

Voice: Wish for the quince as a fruit and eat it, but do not eat from the quinces on the forbidden tree! Every extra bit *of knowledge I give will limit your dreams. You will be out of **Dreammatic** if you eat the QUINCE. It is a reward to be here for some while it's a nightmare for others.*

Is there an opposite of Dreammatic, a Fearmatic where my fears become a reality? I don't know, but I don't really care. I just want to discover the limits of *Dreammatic* and enjoy it for now. 'LET THERE BE my deceased father, grandmother and grandfathers here with me...'

My environment suddenly changed into my grandmother's house in Edirne while all three of them appeared before me. Nonplused, I went ahead and hugged them. They also hugged me as we fulfilled our longing for each other in tears. After a short talk about how we had been doing, they stared at my face with affectionate eyes when I started to ask questions like 'You are in Heaven, right?'. I couldn't get any answers but only the affectionate looks and touches.

After they asked how school was, how my friends were doing and if I ate my meal regularly or not, I realized that I was precisely reliving the moment of union we had when I came to Edirne for the first semester's holiday in my student years in Ankara.

Did this Dreammatic try to distract me by making me relive the most emotional memory record in my brain?

It was wonderful to meet with my family elders even though it was in Dreammatic and fulfill my longing eventhough it was a dream. Only unless you are drown in this swamp of helplessness feeling this old and deep indescribable longing in you once you wake up...

(The voice intervened all of a sudden.)

Voice: Dreammatic is a setting of individual experiences. You can not bring anybody here with his real soul, who is still alive or has been alive before. You can create their counterparts from the memory records in your memory, you can live the once lived memories repeatedly but you cannot bring the memory itself.

(This initial sentimentalism was over and I felt myself totally lonely.) **If there is no sentimentalism, no family, no friends in Dreammatic, and if everything and everyone except me is illusion, and if there will never be real love and real passion, then how could one be happy here by himself?**

Voice: Just think of what happens when there are also others with you. Which of them will Dreammatic realize when each of you comes up with a different wish? When your wish comes true, the others would have to live in a dream which was totally defined by you, a dream which they have no voice for. A place whose purpose is to serve happiness and peace will turn into an atmosphere of brawl and cha-

*os. And Dreammatic will turn into the reality of the **old world** in just a few minutes...*

You are right but just imagine that you are an ardent fan; if you are dreaming of a match, you get to choose the opponent and you need to think about the result as well as each step separately. How will I be able to rest and enjoy it while I decide on a number of things that need to be addressed such as the number of the goals, the players who will create the positions, the ones who will score the goals, the referees, the stadium, my seat and the supporters who are with me.

Even if you watch the match from the best seat in the tribune and with all the illusionary supporters that you want to have with you; there will be no excitement since there is no surprise. You will just have with you those illusionary puppets in human disguise which you have created, make up a match with a given result, and become happy watching it and seeing the result, is that it? (Digital illusion, the Dreammatic, in this form, is just like a fantasy machine which responds to mundane needs. You can be quite happy here as well unless you question its reality. Such an advanced technology couldn't have been created for simple purposes that serve appetite or sexual fantasies. I think one can demand in five areas from Dreammatic: (1) I wanted material things such as house, car, office, yacht and they came true, (2) I saw how it was realized when I wanted my deceased father, grandmother and grandfathers with me as well. There remains (3) The transitions between very crowded settings (4) Learning about the future (5) Wishing for something I have never known or seen before. So I decided to see how each will unfold by saying LET THERE BE for them one by one.)

<u>Wish-4:</u> As I said **'LET ME BE in İstanbul, Taksim Square, at the entrance of İstiklal Street at 11:55 pm on 31st of January 2013.'**, I was in the midst of this crowd whose authenticity and movingness seemed super enthusiastic. All around it was bursting at the seams. Suddenly, the moment I said:

'LET ME BE at the squares where the New Year is celebrated in New York, Paris, London, Sydney, Moscow respectively on 31st of December 2013, with 3 minutes intervals starting from 23:58.' I welcomed the year 2014 in enthusiastic crowds in these cities I wished to be in, in the same order I determined. Everything including the people, the buildings, the music and the sky at the squares were manifesting instantly in a perfect speed with a rich content. You are literally there and you experience it through feeling and with an authenticity that you cannot even doubt of.

My most cherished prayer has always been 'My Lord, Increase My Wisdom!';

<u>Wish-5:</u> As soon as I said **'LET THERE BE masters that will deliver knowledge from the future and increase my wisdom.'** I received an annoyed answer from the Voice.

Voice: What do you think we are? Do you think we are from the first age, the old stone age?

I didn't mean to be bad. Where am I? Whose creation is this life form I am in? Who am I speaking to? I am really curious about the degree and the position of the voice I confer with, with respect to the time line. If I didn't die and come to heaven, then who are you? Are you some beings with some superhuman powers that have overtaken people's brains? Have I been abducted from the Earth and kept captive in another place? Have I been put to sleep in the era I once lived and awakened in the future? Are you the guides? Or am I in a dream created by my own sub consciousness?

Voice: It is pleasing to see that none of your predictions underestimated the power of human beings or attributed the creation and salvation to extraterrestrials. Are you seeking the knowledge or the source? As I told you before, every new piece of information about the identities would restrict you.

Knowledge is like a garment; it both displays and covers at the same time. It can be just like a weed which misleads, by hiding what's essential. You cannot see the body by just looking at the garment.

It would be no different than asking 'Where are you from Professor?' to a teacher who gives a lecture in the class. If you only look at the teacher and focus merely on him, you will miss the knowledge he communicates. Now focus on the knowledge and please **'Do not determine who created it before understanding what it is that you are in!'**

Why would knowledge be restricting me even though I said 'My Lord, increase my wisdom?'

Voice: The source of the knowledge as well as the identity or the position of the person who communicates it all cause serious damage on the learning here. That's to say; **(1)** *In case I say I am a guide and everything I tell is a channeling knowledge, I will take from you the freedom to probe. You will find yourself in a position where you believe without questioning. You will be practicing everything I tell you after directly accepting them.* **(2)** *If I say I am God, you will be too perplexed to do anything and instead of preaching people about me and calling them to faith, you will not help anyone because you will be looking down on them.* **(3)** *If I talk as fire, you won't listen anything I say because you think fire is the Devil.* **(4)** *If I say I am an alien, you will not feel secure and even become a world nationalist. The training will be over and we will start talking about other things.* **(5)** *If I say I am an Illusion, a digital robot, you will ask 'Are you a Digital Guru?' or 'Who is controlling you?'* **(6)** *If I say that I am just a human being like you, you will never believe it and you will think that I am saying this to make you feel comfortable.*

Because of such reasons, we created an illusionary life form which you suppose that you perceive through your five senses. By this way, you will comprehend the knowledge as it is, without the interference of your personal bias. Think of it this way: You go to a seminar and listen the person who gives the seminar talking about his academic titles, the books he has authored and his references written by the authorities one by one. To what extent could your thoughts and questions be free while you are listening to his seminar? His position can put the knowledge in pledge so that no one else except those who hold this position is allowed to make an interpretation about the subject. You will not be able to access any answers for the questions in your mind; just like the lecturer, because of his barriers of 'position' in his mind, will not access the thought-stimulating questions and knowledge he had the chance to access through the questions that would be asked.

Whereas, science should be able to encourage even the people on the streets and make them think ; it should be able to receive their contribution. For instance, cell phone producers have their products tested by every segment in the society and they always learn unexpected new solutions from unexpected people. The identities or statuses are not used during the trainings in this dimension, so that the answers are accessed and it's ensured that the only focus point is the knowledge.

Accordingly, it is ensured that everyone who has a comment or solution gets to express it and such contributions are always listened with attention. Let me illustrate this with a funny example; a man goes to a doctor for the treatment of his insomnia.

Doctor: *'What is the problem?'*

The Man: *'I feel as if there's someone under my bed while I am lying on it. I go under the bed and lie there but this time I have a feeling that there is someone on it. I am dying of sleeplessness switching between the two during the whole night.*

Doctor: *"We can treat it in roughly 6 months, by having a session each week''.*

The Man: *'Alright.' And he leaves. They meet after 4 or 5 months.*

Doctor: *'You look fine. Did you go to another doctor, considering that you didn't come to me?'*

The man: *'I didn't go to another doctor, but I solved the problem for 5 Liras.'*

Doctor: *'I am really curious to know how you solved it.'*

The man: *'I made a calculation after I left your office. I was quite frustrated to find out that the treatment of weekly sessions you offered, each costing 250 TL, meant 24 sessions in 6 months which made a total cost of 5.500 TL. I* *could never pay that. So I decided to go to a cafe and have a tea. Seeing my unhappiness and hopelessness, the waiter asked what the problem was. I told him about my problem, he laughed and said 'Is this really what you are worrying about? Go and buy a saw for 5 Liras, cut the bed legs and you are done.' So I bought a saw and cut the bed legs, I can sleep easily now. There you go, you never know who has the solution or the answer to your problem: you never know where the answers are hiding. If you can just get over your bias and arrogance, you can find the practical solutions in everyone, everywhere.*

All of a sudden the environment transformed into a stadium where my favorite team was taking the field. The game was about to start and I had the best seat with some ardent fans. I suddenly started to clap, cherishing the team with great enthusiasm captivated by the excitement in the tribunes. It didn't take me long to realize that I was in the championship match which has been most memorable to me. The scenario, which I was told that I had the authority to change, was evidently being interfered. You know how they always say: 'LIVE THE MOMENT, GO WITH THE FLOW'. I think it's high time, it is time to enjoy those moments in the tribune which I had watched once from the TV. There is no ifs, ands or buts when it comes to my favorite team. Enjoy first and question later. Do not spoil your enjoyment while trying to question!

I became even more enthusiastic when my houris came along and supported my team with me. To my surprise, they also support my favorite team. (What a surprise☺) It was much nicer to watch the same game with these beautiful and warm houris. In order to draw me in its scenarios, Dreammatic was adding new sections that I would love to experience.

After a while, the excitement I felt when I thought of what I would do with these beautiful girls after the match became more interesting than the excitement I felt more the match.

These illusionary houris who did not belong to anyone, were so real that eventhough you knew you were deceived by the perceptual blows you had, created by their uplifting looks, touches and kisses, you can't help feeling this excitement. They are fake but what they make you feel is real. What a challenging contradiction…

As expected, I fast-forwarded the game because I got bored of watching a match whose result I knew. We jumped in my roadster and drove to my mansion after having a championship tour in the city. Although I knew that the houris were the illusions created by my imaginative world, I was dying to try their degree of realness only with test purposes. ☺

Despite I screamed during the match, my voice wasn't hoarse at all. There was no tiredness either, just like they said before, so I stayed up all night feeling still very ener-getic. I wish I could have thought of this tribune thing while I was in the world life. I would have sold it as a pro-ject to all the TV companies, teams or concert organizers. Just think how terrific it would be to watch the game or the concert optionally from a private lodge or amongst the fans in the tribune only by using 3-D glasses while you are still home. I can watch the concerts, other sports competitions and any other live broadcasting in 3-D wherever I want, with all the supporters I like and live the excitement with them. It is a reality integration provided only by 3-D glass-es and earphones without even the requirement of a televi-sion. Live broadcast would not only be live broadcasting any more but there would also be a JAL 'Just Like Live' written at the corner of the screen. I can sell this to a TV channel, a TV producer or an advertising agency when I go back to the world. Anyway, it's senseless to think about worldly things here.

Now, I would like to try this choice (6th) choice. I was re-ally curious to know its consequence. If it's true that every-thing just shapes as I like, let's see how this Dreammatic works when I wish for something that I have never seen or known before. I had watched this game from home. How was I able to imagine that I watched this game from the tribune even though this tribune scene wasn't found in my memory records? I guess they imagined it instead of me. Could Dreammatic give me what's beyond my dreams?

THERE IS NOWHERE BUT WHERE YOU ARE
AND NO ONE BUT THOSE WHO ARE THERE

<u>Wish-6:</u> The moment I said **'LET THERE BE a house that I own on a glacier in the polar region which I have never seen or known before!'**, I was right there in this house on the glacier. **How was this place created which was not found in my memory records at all?**

*Voice: You are right. Your ability to imagine is limited by your knowledge. Through the recollections recorded in your memory, we very well know what you have seen or haven't seen before. Yet what we know is not limited by your memory records. In our memory archive, there are also the memory records of those people who have discovered this region and been there before. The records of knowledge and experience of all the other people are registered, juts like yours is, in the Central Database, which we call the **Collective Memory.** A glacier record that you haven't seen or known before was detected in the Collective Memory and the house was created on it, that's all!*

The tribune scene you had was also taken from the memory records of someone that watched the same match from the best seat in the tribune. His eyes became your eyes, his ears became you ears. The vocal and visual records taken from his eyes and ears have been delivered to your visual and auditory cortices. His eyes, his ears have become ONE with your soul and you watched the match. He almost became You and You became Him. Think of it this way; if you know somebody's entire past, that means you know what makes him happy and you can offer him surprisal happy moments without needing to ask him any-

thing about himself. Just as when your mother makes you happy when she cooks your favorite dish as a surprise...(It is a food for thought to reckon that the system which knows you so well has also the chance of making you very unhappy as well.)

What happened to my house by the seaside and my work place with the bosphorus view? Are they still there in their place?

*Voice: Your house and your workplace, together with everything in their environment have disappeared and they will not be there until you say 'LET THERE BE' for them to appear once again. I can give you an example; imagine that you are walking in a city whose motion-sensitive streets are equipped with lamps that work with illumination sensors. The street you enter will be il-luminated while the lamps on the street you leave will be off since there is no motion there any more. Whichever way you go, the only lighted street will be the one you are found at that mo-ment and the other streets will be dark. Just like in the dream, **there is nowhere but where you are, and no one but those who are there.***

Considering the logic of these sensor streets, was it the pre-vious house that turned into this one? Or is the previous house still there while this one is located in another region of Dreammatic? What will happen to this house if I want to turn back to the seaside again? Will it revive on the glacier while this one becomes desolated here?

Voice: You aren't in a place made of matter, but you are in a place of illusion which seems like matter. Imagine that you are making a splendid sand castle on a beach. Your castle made of sand, which is a reflection of your spirit, will stay there at the beach if you don't destroy it and wait there and watch it, fixing the disfigured parts. In case you destroy it or leave the beach, the wind and the rain will dispel it and take back the sand particles into the wholeness of the sand. Each sand particle will be a part of the sand wholeness once again.

Later, someone else comes and makes statues of sand on the same beach which is smoother now. And the very sand particles that you used for your castle, become an animal, a plant or a human statue in his sand statues. When he leaves, the sand particles he used in his statues turn back into the wholeness of the sands. Then another and another person comes and they all make the reflections of their soul using the same sands of the same sand wholeness. Just as you used some sand particles that have been used by others in their statues before... The sand wholeness will grant its sands to the order of your soul only for a certain period of time so that you can make the statue or castle that you like. Through this transformation, the surface of the beach takes a shape for a while but then it becomes flat and then re-shapes again. The sands in the wholeness of the beach are given under the order of the souls within the framework of the basic principles and then they take form depending on the thoughts of these souls.

Isn't it true for the earthly bodies of humans as well? Our bodies, just like sands on the beach, consist of billions of cells that come together in one place. You bring together billions of cells by eating vegetables, fruits, plants and animals found in the Earth wholeness and you form your earthly body. Then you control the body you form and keep it as a shadow of your soul on earth. When your soul leaves your body, the process begins for your body to turn back to the earth wholeness. Your cells merge with the soil and become nourishment for an animal, plant or a tree. Your cells become parts of various different living bodies and begin to serve these souls. A cell may sometimes become a part of an animal while it is a part of a human at other times. The cells have been repeating this cycle for millions of years and of course, as a part of a different body in each different time. Mankind makes houses, cars, airplanes, tables and chairs by bringing together the atoms on earth. Later, as these become non-utilizable, they first become the atoms which turn back to the matter wholeness. Then they become the parts of other goods repeatedly through wreckage or other ways that we call re-cycling. This recycling on earth, which is a closed box in itself has been continuing this way for millions of years. Each cell experiences utterly different lives and bodies each time they are in a human, an animal or a plant body. You say that there's a separate beach for each person and that the same cycle in each of them. Remembering the concept of evolution in Rumi's writings: 'I was the stone, the soil. I died and became a plant. I died and became an animal. I died and I became human.'

What happens to the soul when the body disappears?

*Both the matter and the soul are inclined to go back to their original wholeness. The spirit goes back to the home of the spirits, the spiritual wholeness so to speak. This is also how Dreammatic works. You can create and direct anything you want, animate/inanimate, like soil, stones, forests, animals, plants and humans, only by dreaming of them. If you get out of Dreammatic or say **'LET THERE BE'** for something new, the existing reality disappears and a new scenery gets established according to your new wish. The scenes disappear in themselves and re-appear at any time. Just like on the TV or computer screen, the existing reality is reset and then recreated in a speed* *of thought, and you can't follow the transition between. It is no different than the light bulb which blinks 50 times in a second; all the scenes disappear and reappear again in a speed that you fail to comprehend.*

What do not disappear is the spirit and the knowledge. The sand castle you make on the beach is dispersed and turns back to the sand wholeness. You assume that it is gone but the traces of the records, which we call memories, that it left in the soul as well as in Dreammatic never disappear and are all recorded as a permanent archive in the Collective Memory.

Isn't it the same when a person adds something emotional of himself to a painting, a shoe or a food whether it's an artist, housewife or someone from another profession? The artifacts and names of those who do their work with love by adding a spirit of their own and creating an awareness, are always transferred to the next generation as an inspiring knowledge.

Those people add so much love to their work that if it's a shoe, it becomes something more than a shoe; if they are socks they become something beyond simple socks. Whether it's a shoe, a dress, some socks or something to eat; they all turn into a work of art as becoming the extension of these people's soul and the love they felt for what they did. We name them like artisan Mehmet Ali's shoes or Melahat's pasta etc... We want to promote, preserve and protect these works which have been created with love. The effort shown by these artists influence the eras ahead of them and they create awareness with their enlightening results. So we ensure that the coming generations see and take them as examples.

UNIVERSAL TELEPATHY AND COLLECTIVE MEMORY

The words of Aşık Veysel, 'I leave but my name remains, let the friends remember me', makes me question if the update for new information transferred only to the new born. Is it not transferred to the others?

Voice: What we call Universal Telepathy, which is the foundation for what you name as the Entanglement Theory, is the simultaneous communication achieved between the pieces of the same group objects that are in distant places, through the invisible, mysterious long distance connections called the ghost links. This system which we can call as the online information update; is valid for animals, humans and all the living beings. An impact on one of them will cause the same results on all the others.

The monkeys in different continents thousands of miles apart from one another are all connected to the Collective Memory. The memory records of each monkey are kept in the monkey's section in the Collective Memory. When one of the monkeys learns to crack a crusty fruit using a stone, the others belonging to the same category and live in other parts of the world have an update of information simultaneously through the memory links in the Collective Mind.

These invisible memory links exist between humans as well. Your mother, father, grandmother, grandfather, siblings, aunts, nephews and nieces are your immediate family members, each of them becomes a mother, father, sibling, nephew, aunt or uncle to some other people whose relatives will eventually become others' relatives as well. Briefly, each and every other human is a relative to one another biologically, in a direct or indirect way, and any action taken by one, or anything one of them gets exposed to, will have an influence on all the other people and actually every other living being.

Each person is an individual, in the family of humanity and gets affected, consciously or unconsciously, by all the happiness and unhappiness experienced by other individual family members.

That's why the babies born with a basic memory updated with new information in the Collective Mind adapt themselves to new technologies much quicker than the adults, if they're given the chance. Potentially, everyone has the chance to access any information in the memory but they can only access to those sections that they are allowed to. This scope of authority and influence may expand or contract in time.

You can call anyone on the phone but you don't necessarily reach each of them, do you? What kind of chances does the Collective Memory present to me in the face of new incidents?

***Voice:** Think of it this way, when you face an incident, you are being presented all the positive and negative choices that you created in the Collective Memory including the bombardment of the media/ press, the experiences you had when you faced other incidents and the patterns of the society you live in. You decide which one to choose through your subconscious records.*

<u>Example:</u> You called your wife and she didn't answer! You will think that the chances are: (1) She doesn't have the phone with her. (2) She didn't hear it, she will call as soon as she sees the missed call. (3) She heard it but she wasn't available (she's driving/ she is in the market, in the bathroom) (4) She would always answer, I am sure there's a problem. (5) Who knows what she's up to!... (6) She's having one of these deep conversations with a friend and she forgot everything else. (7) She got my call but she doesn't answer purposely to annoy me. (8) She is with someone that I don't want her to see and she knows that I would be very angry if I hear that. (9) I am sure she's cheating on me!

If you did not have issues of disloyalty before, and you weren't influenced by any negativity you witnessed in other relationships around you or by the stories of cheating constantly brought up in press and media, and neither these influences nor your wife didn't cause insecurity in you towards the opposite sex, you will probably be choosing (1), (2), (3), (4). Whereas, if you don't trust her driving skills or her life experience or if you believe that she is naive or weak and think that she might be deceived, then the choices will be (5), (6), (7), or (8). If there is a trust issue in your relationship originating from you or your spouse, you will probably choose (9). Even a person with a sound judgment can lose his common sense when he acts upon his immediate feelings in the face of an unexpected event. Reason steps back and the conflict fuels his concerns which might turn into serious fears. The choices you make after an unanswered call, eventhough there is no factual data about the event, is the reflection of your subconscious regarding this subject and the level of trust between you and your wife. In case you thought of (9), even if your wife calls ten minutes later and says 'I didn't hear the phone, I just saw your call.' it wouldn't make any difference. The ten minutes silence was an unproved disloyalty for you.

Those who have been cheated before will think of the 9th choice.

Voice: You are right, but not only the cheated but also the cheaters are inclined to think of the same choice. Cheating occurs when you believe in or value something overmuch. When you value illusion more than reality, it hinders your ability to discern that it's illusion.

By the way, since Collective Memory works with the principle of artificial intelligence which is in a constant learning process, when you produce a new different choice about an issue, the Collective Memory will enable it for the service of humanity and begin to present 10 choices, instead of 9. Let's give an example: You are at the entrance of the apartment and your phone rings. You see that it's your wife calling. You are already there about to enter so instead of answering the phone, you want to stand right before her and answer her 'Yes, honey.' when you meet at the door. In this case, when your wife calls and you don't answer, your wife will think 'He should be quite close if he doesn't answer' which will create the 10. choice. From then on, people who face a similar situation will be presented with a set of pos-

sibilities which consist of 10 choices. The Collective Memory is the Collective Memory of all humanity, the statuses or positions are totally irrelevant in this case; anyone can contribute to another through his experiences. The internet, through which millions of people ask questions and record something every second, is the most primitive form of the Collective Memory. You instantly reach numberless sources of information related to your research.

That means, we are all directly connected to the Collective Memory.

Voice: We are directly and continuously on-line. Just as Murat KIRHAN told you, you don't give any identity information in your prayers such as 'God, I am Aydın Türkgücü from İstanbul, Turkey, my ID number is...' Because you know that God knows you directly. So you go ahead and express your request. That is also how you are connected to the Collective Memory; directly and on-line. Prayer is a person's effort to change and reprogram the reality. He knows that he is able to do it in his very essence yet it might take a long time for him to understand and use that Divine power.

Just like a TV broadcasting; there are different types of programs in hundreds of TV channels and I watch whichever I choose depending on my mood. If I want to make a contribution to the existing choices, I should launch a new TV channel and design a new TV program.

Voice: You don't need to launch a new channel or produce a TV program in order to make a contribution to the Collective Memory. You may only bring in a new episode for a TV series or a TV program; or just create a new subject, a new line to one of the characters; a new design for the decor or furnishing. Briefly, let it be something new that you have started. Everything you do is you yourself, except the things you have learnt. And even the slightest contribution is taken seriously. If you want to make a contribution, you should take a different approach than those before you, to what you are already offered. If you only approach just like they did, you will naturally end up with the same results and will have repeated them.

Considering that the Collective Memory consists of the knowledge and experience which mankind has collected over thousands of years, then is there only the past? What about the future?

Voice: Think of it this way: once you learn the addition, subtraction, multiplication and division in nature, you can easily deal with any kind of mathematical operations in life such as shopping, product purchase or payments. But remember, the man has even accomplished to go to the space by going beyond what he has already known by discovering new mathematical models like the integrals or differential equations from what he knew? Therefore, what you know has been given for you to find and attain many things that you do not know yet. Knowledge is the most important tool, your dreams can only reach up to the extent of your knowledge. There are also these sections which use advanced future modeling, what is future for you and is past for us. In that case, in order to reach the level of advanced knowledge and experience in the Collective Memory, you should learn about the knowledge and experiences that are prior to you. You don't think you can reach the final stage before going through the phases and challenges many has passed through before, do you? Think of it as a school: you can't take on the duty from the previous ones before you complete all the classes and applied internship and graduate. Anyone who gets to complete his training, may take charge as an educator or practitioner in his subject in the Collective Memory.

It is almost like a rally racing. That's exactly what I would like to have as a duty, being computer programmer: to be in the team which writes the new versions in the Collective Memory. Did you send those people from your team who changed the history through the charges they had taken in the world?

Voice: It would be a serious underestimation of their intelligence, intuitive abilities and efforts to show their success as some hormonal achievements and to name them as people in charge whom we sent or who acted according to the commands we gave.

The Collective Memory is virtually an internet directed by telepathically thoughts. Why is it so obligatory and important?

Voice: The memory is the section that stores what you know. Take notice that your knowledge is determined by your memory, not by the extent of your intelligence. If you don't have the memory, the knowledge in other words, your intellect and your talents are ineffectual. The patients who have Alzheimer's disease can not do anything at the peak of their knowledge and experience, in a time they can make the best of their mind, because they do not remember what they repeated many times before due to the disconnection with their memory. Once you connect with the Collective Memory, you can directly reach your own memory as well as all the sections available to you that were recorded. In that case, you will have enlargened your own memory thousands or millions of times. You can think of it as a mental internet you can connect directly with your brain and ask questions.

Well, if everything I experience is recorded in the Collective Memory and I can have access to this archive, then why can't I remember everything?

Voice: Imagine you have a phone line in which you have record-ed all your conversations. You normally forget about the details of the conversation after a while later. You need to record the conversation and listen to it from time to time in order not to forget. Repeating is important for the knowledge to be stored for a long time in the brain's own working system that we call the Individual Memory. Each memory has a different retention pe-riod depending on the perceptual and emotional influence the event has created on you. The ones you don't repeat get to be forgotten and thrown into the trash can.

There is also an emotional or psychological aspect of recording. People tend to forget especially about their unpleasant memory records and they usually forget them in the long term. You may change the degree of importance given to a specific event in the archives of your Personal Memory. And sometimes you might want to attribute too much value to a relationship in order to be able to ignore something else in your life. You use it to cover the things you want to ignore. Your friends might say, '... How could something that was so meaningless when you were living it become so precious once it came to an end?' and they won't make sense of it. What they can't see is what you are covering up with it.

A record that was erased because its precedence has changed, will never be erased in the Collective Memory. Think of it this way, you hear noises coming from outside while you are listening the lesson in the classroom. You miss what the teacher is saying because of the distraction. You are in the classroom according to the camera in the class and the witnesses there. You saw the teacher and you heard what she was saying. However, since your brain was preoccupied with something else, it recorded 'what it just saw and heard' directly in the category of the unimportant things without making any sense of them. It is no different than missing what is discussed in a meeting because of daydreaming. Sometimes, someone comes and asks you 'Do you remember how we used to play snowball when we were children. But we haven't seen one another since I moved to another city.' But you don't even remember the person, let alone playing snowball with him.

In this case I would think it wasn't that important. I would have remembered it if it was. Why does the Collective Memory record everything? Wouldn't it save a serious amount of space if it just recorded the important ones?

Voice: The details of an event which seem meaningless today, might be very important in the future and you might regret that you had not recorded them. Think of it this way; let's say you are working in a hospital and you keep the records of the names, surnames, id numbers, the name of the illnesses and the phone numbers of the patients and their results of the urinalysis and blood analysis. Years later, the statistics are required to find out the subfactors of the illness. If you don't have the information about the sex, age, smoking habits, marital status, birth place, the schools etc, the effort you showed to keep the records of all the other information will not serve any purpose. In short, an event might be crucial for the humanity while it doesn't seem important to you at all. On the contrary, something which seems very important to you might be trivial for humanity.

Remember what we discussed: someone comes and says to you: 'We used to play snowball with you when we lived in the same neighborhood once we were children. But we haven't seen each other again after I moved to another city.', and you don't remember anything about that time. Is she lying? How would you solve this puzzle?

I would call my childhood friends from my childhood and ask them. If they don't remember either, then she should be lying. If they do, then it's only me who doesn't remember it. How else could you solve this puzzle? Ooooor, the Sacred Archive! I would check my records in the Collective Memory. They are all recorded there anyway.

I would accept what she is saying without trying to find any witnesses because a visual document is an evidence I couldn't object. Why don't we use these records in courts? We would stop praying for the judge to read the file and understand the truth. Why do we still have the courts if there is such a technology?

Voice: There surely are reasons for them but these are the subjects of Thinkmatic and we will talk about them in due time. Do you have any other questions about here?

Just as you said, I can't help getting curious about Thinkmatic and I am distracted.

Voice: Here, everything is a test for what has been said previously. That's living the moment and making it live. Not only your untimely predictions based on some missing information about the past which you can't change or the future which hasn't taken place yet, will be unreal, but they will also be of no use for this moment. Now, use your attention to learn the limits and secrets of this place so that you will deserve to go Thinkmatic.

Considering that you are telling about some limits, what would happen if I said LET THERE BE in Dreammatic for something that hasn't been recorded in the Collective Memory yet?

Voice: In this case, the module of scenario-completing will take over. By using the existing knowledge, it will select the most probable choices amongst the possibilities. Why are you anxious?

As one of the laws which are known as Murphy Laws, Edward A. Murphy Jr. says *'If your attack is going really well, it's an ambush!'*. I began to think the same about Dreammatic. There is no difference between thinking and speaking in Dreammatic. You can directly decode the digital signals produced by my brain as I am thinking or speaking. You are almost closer to me than my jugular vein. This Dreammatic where everything happens as you wish and everything gets recorded fully may not have been created only as a reward.

Furthermore; one should not know or understand that he's in an illusionary settings of Dreammatic to be happy in this digital illusion which captivates his visual memory. It seems like there is no point in staying in this illusionary setting where there are only unreal places, people, emotions and an

unreal love. One needs to get out of the illusion as soon as possible in order to see the real. I saw the forbidden tree and its forbidden quinces while I was thinking 'Where is this QUINCE tree...'.

Voice: You are rejecting this place where anything you might want including money, women, food, travel manifests as you wish, are you? Don't you think you gave in too quickly?

The way out of an illusionary system should be ignoring what the system offers you. Just as you said, all I want just manifests but things I might ask for are generally the things which I would define as ego and they are mundane needs or bodily pleasures that harm my soul. Moreover, I would call this 'solving' rather than 'giving in'.

Voice: That's interesting! What is it that you solved? I am really curious to hear it...

The most important thing I solved is to see that Dreammatic is not a favorable place for me. Dreammatic draws people into the labyrinth of a limitless fake happiness by learning their needs from their memory records and creating special scenarios and illusionary actors. If it's only a remotely controlled illusionary puppet that I will experience love with, Dreammatic is over for me. I need to get out of here as soon as possible. Moreover, it really disturbs me to talk to a voice.

Considering that anything I want manifests, I said '**LET the voice that speaks to me BE visible**'. A woman after my own heart just appeared before me. Who came in was a woman eventhough the voice was male. We greeted one another. While I was thinking that this should be an illusionary bait to keep me in the Dreammatic, the Voice intervened as I asked '**Who are you?**'

Voice: This woman is your soulmate that you have been looking for in Thinkmatic. Your soulmate appears when you reject the false happiness that is offered to you. This is an automatic procedure. You need to renounce the false one in order to reach the real. She would appear anyway if you just said 'LET my soulmate BE incarnated in a human body, right near me'. You might have wanted to stay more in the Dreammatic then. Just think about it, it's a perfect place for the women, with countless dresses, numberless shoes, SPA, cosmetics, invaluable jewelry etc which are all free.'.

My soul mate interrupted, 'I reject! None is for me, thanks.' She held my hand saying 'Come on honey, let's get out of here.' And we were right under the QUINCE tree. This woman should definitely be my soulmate if I think of her ability to direct my scenes. She hugged me and we had a long kiss feeling these delightful emotions that one feels when he is kissing the woman he loves. When we stopped, she plucked a forbidden quince off the tree that would annihilate the boundary between the truth and us. Handing it to me, she said: 'You need to eat in order to know...'

Voice: Are you sure that you just didn't rise to the bait and decide hastily, namely following a fait accompli presented by your soulmate? How do you know that she's your soulmate? Are you sure that she's not one of the illusionary puppets that you have just looked down on? Are you sure that you have measured all the limits and secrets of Dreammatic? Are you sure that you have found and understood all the answers in it and demanded *and experienced everything for which you could have said **'LET THERE BE'**?*

(As I held my soulmate tightly around her waist, kissing her passionately and feeling a complete union of spirit and body)

'She's definitely my soulmate, I can understand that!' I said. There is new knowledge and more answers outside than there are inside. Just as you said a while ago, I need to renounce the false completely in order to reach the real.

(Holding her hand, I put he QUINCE right between our lips so that we can bite it together. And when we were just about to bite the QUINCE looking into each other's eyes…)

Voice: Are you saying that such a technology that creates the houses or the women of your dreams cannot create your love kiss? This was a good training in learning the consequences of making someone the center of your life, before you understand who or what she is. Now, I ask you again, did you experience everything that you have said LET THERE BE for, did you reach the limits and the secrets of Dreammatic? Why are you in a hurry, do you know where this exit will lead to? You may not come back once you are out. Can not the power that controls the senses be controlling the emotions as well?

The voice was right. A technology that can control the senses could easily control the emotions as well. Recognizing these questions as a warning, I changed my abrupt decision about eating the QUINCE and began contemplating.

I didn't sail in my boat but that isn't important at all. I didn't work in my company or produce new ideas but I can do this better outside with new knowledge and new answers. Actually there was something that I didn't ask. **'Can I take anything to outside? Like a ring on my finger, a watch on my wrist?**

Voice: My answer is both 'yes' and 'no'. You cannot take away anything material but you will remember the experiences you gained. You can't bring in anything or take away anything material from here. Can you literally take something material from your real world into your dreams or take it from your dreams to bring it into the real world? Do you get up feeling full when you eat in your dream or do you wake up as a rich person if you win the lottery in your dream?

No, because you cannot bring in or take away anything material in a mental place. It works the same way it does in the world; you cannot bring anything physical when you are coming into the world just as you can't take anything with you when you are leaving the world. When you get out of Dreammatic and wake up, what remains will only be the knowledge and experience you had here, just like the case in your dreams. Waking up means realizing, being enlightened in this context. Knowledge and experience are more valuable than anything else.

(How many would go through such an experience in a conscious way when he is in Dreammatic and remember everything when he gets out? There is no need to hurry up, is there? It might be painful for me to get out of here untimely with a lacking knowledge and experience if I can not come back. It is similar to fail in an exam which you enter with a lack of training, having left the class early by saying 'this is enough for me'. And I don't want to be one of those who say 'I wish I had another chance to turn back to Dreammatic'. And is this woman my soulmate? Or was it an urgent hug that I was expected to have with the first person I saw and thought real amongst the illusionary puppets? I decided to have a little tour.)

I said: **'LET all the wishes I made HAPPEN respectively once again, each for three minutes.'** They all took place starting from the first one, each for three minutes. I remembered that I didn't taste the milk flowing in the river of milk at my work place, but it wouldn't be a realistic test to do that in a setting where my sense of taste was 100% dominated. Then I suddenly saw my spaceship. Yes, I should have definitely experienced this space travelling although it is only an uploading of the memories from the Collective Memory into my own memory. After I went through my wishes once again, I realized that the only thing I still haven't tried was travelling with my space rocket and I said to the Voice;

'Will I be able to do the space travel having more knowledge and again with your guidance, after I get out of Dreammatic? If I can, then I prefer to do it once I am out.

Voice: 'Yes you can do it with more knowledge out of Dreammatic.'

WHY IS THIS LONELINESS?

After all, this place is an illusion based on what I know and it takes shape according to my mind.

Voice: Owning a house on the glacier was something that didn't exist in your mind; it was created from the records in the Collective Memory. This was a totally new experience for you.

You are right, it's said 'the mind cannot be found using the faculties of the mind but through bypassing them.' The reason I wished a house on the glacier was to understand how Dreammatic worked. Zen philosophy suggests 'The solution is not in my mind.' So if Dreammatic is my mind, then the higher knowledge which has the solution must be out of Dreammatic. Isn't there anyone else except me indeed? Are they all illusions while I am the single reality? But why is this loneliness?

Voice: It's very hard to accept but unfortunately it's all illusion except you. These are your limitations and your imaginative world. There are no such things here like judgments, disapprovals, exclusions or punishments. The level of your responsibility is the same as you would have in a dream, you have no responsibility in other words. Just like in your dreams, you don't harm anyone in reality and the cost of these scenes are scarcely any. Here, there is only your ego, without even a second one, and it's not a fault or sin to pursue it.

Why isn't there a second ego, a second person in other words?

Voice: A second ego would cause comparing, a competition. By provoking or frightening you, it will lead you to be more or less than what you really are. You will only be yourself where there isn't any competition. In Dreammatic it is provided that the person reaches her own natural self through a private interactive illusionary model that is totally dependant on instinctual reactions.

It's a happiness machine, an illusion that will make you very happy unless you question its source. Since I am conscious and I am in contact with you, what I see loses its meaning. This saying 'Dying before death' is almost realized as 'killing before death'. It seems like there is everything but there isn't really. You see that they are not there in reality, maybe not even your body, as soon as you understand the illusion. You are virtually dead before death.

Voice: You are right, when the visible material universe loses its reality and becomes an unreliable illusion, you think it has no meaning any more. But you can be sure that it becomes ever more important in time. Because dying before death, understanding where you are coming from and where you are going by realizing the actual death before dying physically is establishing a direct contact with the Creator or the director. Think of this on a chessboard; whether it's the king, queen, knight, bishop or the pawn, they have no meaning at all before the game starts. But when they are lined on the chess board representing another player who will play against you, which represents the opponent and the game becomes important to an extent that you might be surprised to see. The level of importance changes when it's a casual game or if it's a competition. They are just pieces of stones once the game is over because the matter is valueless and meaningless if there is no one to direct it.

They were all stones in nature before a stone mason gave them shape and made them into chessmen. Just as the man shapes up his soul through Dreammatic and Thinkmatic...

EXITING DREAMMATIC and FREE WILL

Who has the control behind the life model in Dreammatic? Following your advice *'Do not determine who created it before understanding what it is that you are in!',* **I would like to learn about the secrets and the limits of the Dreammatic itself, rather than seeing the secrets and the limits of my own mind in Dreammatic,**

I held my soulmate's hand suddenly. God explicitly told Adam and Eve that they would be expelled from heaven if they ate the forbidden fruit. It is interesting that they ate the forbidden fruit of the forbidden tree of knowledge anyway, despite this explicit warning.

Voice: You are right but they kept begging and begging to turn back, being remorseful of their exit. Be careful not to have the same remorse they had!

If you say to man that nothing is forbidden except this fruit and that's the only ban you impose, then you condemn him to this choice. The penalty of exclusion eating the forbidden fruit make people question 'What is there out of the Dreammatic that I should know? Why would be the founders of Dreammatic uneasy if I learn this?' Now, show me something that will make me happy, that's is worth staying here so that I will stay.

Voice: There's a Divine hint in every Divine knowledge. Isn't it a clear evidence of free will granted to mankind for his each step, to give Adam the chance to choose freely in Heaven? Was it not a practice of free will when Satan did not prostrate when God commanded that all the angels prostrate Adam? Free will denotes a choice you make freely. There is no penalty if there is no free will. It is your free will, your free choice to eat or not to eat the quince. Do not defend yourself in vain by saying that your soulmate has deceived you.

If my soulmate is real, she will be with me when I am out, just as in the scenario of Adam and Eve. (Let the man make the woman eat the forbidden fruit, I thought, inspired by Yunus Emre.)

As I was saying, **'It is just a few illusionary girls and a few houris what they call Dreammatic, let those who lust for them take them; all I need is you, and you only......'** I put the QUINCE between the mouths of us in a way that we can bite at once. I counted 1-2-3 looking into her eyes and bit the forbidden fruit.

It all went dark as I did. I guess I was in my bed and my soulmate wasn't with me. My adventure that began in utter darkness ended up in utter darkness. I first decided to look for my soulmate feeling that I was standing on this fine line between hope and hopelessness. With my trembling voice, frightened to be left unanswered, I asked: 'Where are you my dear darling?'

No reply, unfortunately. Did she not bite the quince? Did she stay in Dreammatic? Or was she an illusionary houri created to expel me from the Dreammatic by taking advantage of the weakness I felt because of my emotional loneliness and soulmate obsession. No, no I can't say that. They told me 'Don't hurry up, are you sure that your soulmate is not an illusion?' This time, all I could ask to the Voice was: 'Are we out of Dreammatic?'

Again, there was no answer. I was feeling this bitter remorse people had when they really understand the value of something or someone that they didn't care or know at all until they lose it. I had no chance but to accept this bitter reality where non-response was the answer itself…

No, I shouldn't give in! How could you enter into a place where you exit only when you bite the Quince?

I immediately closed my eyes, thinking that the only way back to Dreammatic training should be going back to sleep and dream before I start to feel more awake. But I was totally panicked and it was impossible to sleep after feeling this excitement. The only way to understand if I was really in my room was to turn on the lamp near my bed. I reached out for the lamp. Damn it, the lamp was there. I am in my room and that's my bed. I felt a serious hesitation to press the 'on' button of the lamp, which would prove that all I have seen and heard were a part of a dream. I didn't want to be rash this time and it really didn't seem a good choice to illuminate a darkness for the first time ever. I understood that I had no other chance than turning the lamp on after a moment of resistance and I pressed the button with my eyes closed.

I felt the room being illuminated eventhough my eyes were closed. I half-opened them, not wanting to see at all. What a huge remorse, what an immense pain it was to wake in my bed, having left Dreammatic hastily to reach new answers…

There should be a few quinces in the refrigerator, would it be a reverse journey if I eat it at once? Or should I find a quince tree and eat from the tree? What can I do? I should think positive, I am still in Dreammatic and I am in a scene which makes me experience a remorse prepared well for those like me who make an untimely exit without showing regard to the warnings and exit before completing their trainings like me. The simplest way to understand if I was still in Dreammatic was to wish for something new.

As I said **'LET the Voice BE visible!'** I lost all my hopes upon this painful silence which hurt me so deep in the heart. I ate the quince and there was no way back. Just as it was said, I was dreadfully remorseful.

I guess I was just having one of those guiding dreams that I used to have from time to time. And I had been the student who walked out of the class hastily, saying 'That's enough for me' to reach more. All I could do was to keep the record of this dream which I remembered moment by moment, make it into a book and share it with people right away.

THE FEMALE ENERGY OF THE UNIVERSE: HEAVEN

I should immediately find my computer and write down everything before I forget them. Where is my computer, where is it? It must be in the living room.That's one of the disadvantages of living alone, you need to get up and look for everything for yourself. I went out of the room hurriedly. I did not want to forget about some details while I was busying myself to find the computer. I went into the living room. Aaaand….! Oh my God, what's that!!!

There is a woman in the living room that I don't know. After exchanging glances:

The woman: *Be careful or you will lose your mind. Calm down and breathe deeply. Don't worry, you are safe. You just can't make sense of what you are going through by using the classical knowledge of reality that belongs to the **world dimension based on perception**. Unfortunately there is no other way to explain this any simpler to those who leave the Dreammatic early. Just think that you are still in the dream.*

(perplexed, I tried to ask, stammering)

'So-so-so sorry wh-who-who are you?'. With a sly smile on her face, she spoke with the sonorous voice of the man in Dreammatic: **'I am HIM, remember you said 'let the Voice be visible.'** It is now…

Who is 'He', which He?

Woman: *I am the feminine energy of the universe. Do you think you can go up to the higher dimensions without me? Can you fly with a single wing?*

Can someone not fly without having a feminine energy?

Woman: Can he? Of course he can't. Not just individually but also collectively, it's not possible to fly that way. If you don't believe it, just consider the situation in those countries that ignore, exclude or do not educate their women. Can they rule them-

selves? The woman represents the mother earth in the Holy Scriptures and in the ancient knowledge. You reap what you sow. God created Adam together with Eve. He wouldn't create Eve if there was no need for the female energy. Didn't you come out after the energies of your father (male) and mother (female) came together? And it is not enough for them to come together, they should also be balanced, compatible in other words. Otherwise you cannot fly but only flutter with incompatible wings.

How could man flourish and glow by himself, when in nature not even a single flower wouldn't blossom without male and female energies coming together in nature? In the words of Rumi, 'Each of us is an angel with one single wing and we shall only fly by embracing one another.'

Is there real love in the world dimension?

Woman: Assuming that there is no love, means renouncing the feminine energy. Just as you reach the original when you renounce the false; you get involved with the false when you renounce the real. If you don't ask this question to yourself 'Is it the pain I feel for 'being without you' that drives me, or the loneliness?', you will be lost on the darkest paths, being dragged away by the illusion swamp made of twisty love and happiness that you think is good for your loneliness, and end up somewhere so far from love.

How should I address you?

Heaven: *Heaven, my name is Heaven!*

That's a beautiful name.

Heaven: *You look too surprised for someone who has said 'The women are the gates of Heaven' years ago.*

Is my soulmate in Dreammatic an illusion? It is curious to meet a lady called Heaven after Dreammatic. Why Heaven?

Of course your soulmate was an illusion and it was for your training about the principle 'you reach the original once you renounce the false.' What is there to see in Heaven? Smiling houris, palaces, mansions, delicious food... If you can earn a woman's love, her heart and her respect, and if you also love and respect her in return;

- *She will make you so happy that you wouldn't even turn back to look at those houris when you see them in heaven. You will only want her.*

- *She will manage the house so perfectly that it becomes a happy home. You wouldn't even turn back to look at the most luxurious mansions, villas or palaces.*

- *She will cook and prepare your food with such an affection that it would be so hard for you to eat anything that she didn't prepared.*

You may choose to have these with your woman. But you may also choose to keep her away from everything which would be choosing the hell on earth. You will keep praying for the illusionary houris, beautiful places and delicious food in Dreammatic. Most importantly, as someone who did not experience real love, you will not be able to find the keys of the unseen which you could have found when you were with your woman. I am the female energy that will give a man experience the heaven on earth and enable him to fly by bringing equilibrium to his life.

You are saying that 'in order to be happy, it is not important where you are but who you are with.' Why are you in the living room and not in my room?

Heaven: I chose the living room since you didn't specify a place in your wish. Weren't the Adam and Eve made to land on different places on earth? It was planned that way so that you can learn the details when making a wish. And isn't it more fun?

(And now Heaven started to laugh and this time with a female voice. Probably my face couldn't figure out how to react to all the puzzlement I was going through over and over within the last few minutes)

Are we out of Dreammatic? What will happen now? Come on, let's go there again.

Heaven: From now on, you will sometimes be living in Dreammatic and out of it some other times; you will live in both. So you have taken the basic training that you needed. We will continue with the training as far as your knowledge and your limits of dreaming can extend. About entering Dreammatic again; you will be right there as you think of it since Dreammatic is a mental place. First, you look for the answers yourself; and if you can't find them, we will help you through the clues in the events which will inspire you and make you think and dream.

Can anyone do that?

Heaven: Imagining is designing time and space. You cannot dream of anything that you don't know or intuit. In order to de-

sign a place, you need to have been there before or listened about it from someone else or you need to imagine it intuitively by using what you know. Anyone who reads or listens to your journey, can enter into Dreammatic by just dreaming of it using this mental passage that has been opened. He can discover the most recent places in himself as well as in Dreammatic. It is surely of same importance what to imagine in a place where only imagining is sufficient to do everything.

DIMENSION OF NOTHINGNESS= DIMENSION OF BEING

I beg your pardon but I need to ask something. Where am I now? Am I in an inter-section which Rumi speaks of when he says *'The visible appearance implies and represents an evidence for another appearance in the unseen realm, which also had found its shape from another unseen appearance' (2887)*

Heaven: *You are in this place called the dimension of nothingness.*

Where time and space do not exist!

Heaven: *But you are in the dimension of BEING now.*

Am I in the dimension of BEING or the dimension of NOTHINGNESS?

Heaven: *What does 'the dimension of NOTHINGNESS mean?*

A Place where time and space do not exist.

Heaven: Which means?

Which means the place where time and space don't exist. The state of 'NONE knowledge'. The Black Hole of Thought namely…

Heaven: *It is the place where even the possibility of time and space cannot be produced because there is none knowledge about this place. It is the state of **NONE Knowledge**. If we have any knowledge about it we call it the dimension of BE-ING whereas we call it the dimension of NOTHINGNESS or the dimension of NON-BEING if we don't have any knowledge. The dimension of NOTHINGNESS turn into the dimension of BEING once we have the knowledge. In this case, this world which we live in and have the knowledge of becomes the BEING dimension. Take notice that many areas which had been NOTHING-NESS once before like human body, sub-atomic particles, space etc. have become the areas of BEING once they are reached. The NOTHINGNESSes change into the areas of BEING one by one each day, enlarging the boundaries of our dimension. Each person has a different dimension of NOTHINGNESS and BE-ING. Here was a dimension of NOTHINGNESS for you, but now it's a dimension of BEING for you. Considering that what draws the line between BEING and NOTHINGNESS is knowledge, the dimension of NOTHINGNESS is not a place where time and space do not exist but it is the place whose existence hasn't been proven yet since there is no information about it.*

You are talking about the unknown lower NOTHING-NESSes found in the dimension of BEING. It doesn't explain the original NOTHINGNESS in the higher dimension where time and space do not exist.

__Heaven:__ You are talking about the original home of the souls. What is a soul?

It's energy.

__Heaven:__ Energy is a measurable form. If there is a measurable energy, there has to be time and space. For example electricity is like the soul by itself but it cannot exist in a setting where solid/ liquid/ gas or in short the matter does not exist. A place where there are only souls is not necessarily somewhere in which time and space do not exist. What you needed to learn here was that what we call the NOTHINGNESS is only a lack of knowledge. However there is another dimension of NOTHING-NESS.

Another dimension of NOTHINGNESS?

__Heaven:__ It is the state experienced by those who feel that they are a poor drop in the ocean, accepting that what they know is almost nothing compared to what they should know. It is the dimension of NOTHINGNESS where those people live who feel themselves as __NOTHING,__ like a neutral element unable to change anything in the universe. They don't know how powerful, precious and important they are in the whole, due to the blindness of their despair and inability. They don't see the answers right in front of their eyes. Those who live in this dimension don't see that even the ordinary people could change everything, because they seek the answers from those superhumans who are of the higher dimension that has superhuman conditions.

According to another viewpoint, a person can be so very unhappy that neither time, nor space, nothing has any meaning or importance for him. A private dimension of NOTHINGNESS manifests where this person doesn't feel anything about neither the visible nor the invisible time and space. In short, sometimes NOTHINGNESS is the place which is unknown whereas other times, it is a place that doesn't mean anything at all.

It cannot be expected from an ordinary human being to understand the universe whose beginning and end have been founded on the unknown by the superhuman. Why is there such a disproportionate show of power?

Heaven: *There is no point in searching or making material and spiritual sacrifices for something you will not find. The best thing to do is to be powerful, to have a strong voice and pursue the mundane objectives if there isn't a purpose which aims what's beyond the world. This is the stage when the spirit trails along after the visible matter, moves away from the wholeness by becoming mundane and surrenders itself to matter.*

In these periods where the resources are limited due to the growing population, the ego begins to increase its influence. What becomes prominent is to be the strongest and dominating.

And when the anxiety increases the selfishness and chaos, those who fuel the inability and the anxiety in the first place begin to dominate the society through this anxiety. At certain intervals, the organized emotional violence is ensured to be kept on the agenda through scenarios of drought, unemployment, epidemics or even the apocalypse. The answer is included in the question. If the question is the universe, then the answer is also in the universe and just as they say; the answer is best hidden in sight.

Aristotle said: 'The reason which has its reason in itself.' How could something in sight be hidden?

Heaven: Of course by means of limited choices offered to you. A good example would be the following: A man asks as he visits a mental hospital:
'How do you decide if someone should stay in the mental hospital or not?

Doctor:
-   *We fill a bathtub with water. Then we give three things to the patient. A spoon, a cup and a bucket. And we ask how he would choose to empty the bathtub. What would you do?*
The man:
-Oh! I see. A normal person would prefer the bucket. Because it is larger than the spoon and the cup.

- No, says the doctor. A normal person would uncork the bathtub.

As you see; 'Real intelligence is finding the most appropriate solution, not just selecting one of the choices we are offered.' Remember your dreams, they are very real aren't they?

Yes. They are so real that we can only understand that they are not when we wake up.

Heaven: What do you think of the time and space in dreams? Does the calendar hung on the wall or the watch on your wrist in dreams show the date and the hour in the real world? Are the places you go in your dreams real? Are your worship and pray- ers in dreams valid? Who would you be praying to, when you pray for unreal people, places, events and conditions in your dreams? Are you praying to the god of dreams?

Dreams are not real as they are illusionary settings formed in the parts of my brain where dreams are created. The date and the hour in my dreams are never the same with the real world, other than the exceptional cases. If dreams are such places where time and space do not exist like Dreammatic, then the prayers I do in the dream should be going for noth- ing, they are not being taken seriously.

It is very good that you make the connection with Dreammatic. You dream when your eyes are closed. Because you do not see with your eyes or hear with your ears. Are you always in the same body, at the same age and in the same life scenario in your dream? Is there a continuity in your dreams like the soap oper- as? Is each dream another episode?

Of course not! If we compare it to the car races on the com- puter games; it is impossible for me to physically go into the illusionary car on the computer screen. I can use the car at a distance as an extension of my soul by integrating with the game through the computer.

*Heaven: That's very true. Since Dreammatic and the dreams are a kind of light show, which we call illusion , you are present in dreams or in Dreammatic with your **LIGHT BODY**, which is* *an illusion, an extension of your soul, that's integrated to your soul. You control it from a distance just like it is with the remote controlled cars for it is not possible for you to get into your illusionary body. It is like controlling the car in the computer game with a device such as mouse or joystick.*

It is not possible for ordinary people like me to understand these because it requires an advanced level of technological knowledge to understand an advanced technological design created with higher knowledge. Only a very limited number of people can understand that.

Heaven: *Don't worry. Eventhough the Holographic Dimension of Universe is an advanced technological design made with higher knowledge, it has a simple working principle which anyone can understand, apply in his life and contribute to its content. Anyone who gets a basic update of information that doesn't require any expertise or any detailed information, can understand the basic working principles of the system. If the Creator hid the answer in a way that only the men of science or religion can find and understand, then he would have been unfair to ordinary people. Didn't He choose His prophets from the ordinary people in order to encourage them? God of all, should be the God that all can understand.*

Wholeness is a design that gets created when all come together. Each person (mother, father, sister, brother, uncle, aunt, grandmother, grandfather, friend, teacher, neighbor) contributes to completely different sections of the whole. Not everything is for the eye to see or for the ear to hear.

Some things are to be seen with the light of the heart; they can only be seen with the eye of the heart. When someone whose knowledge has been updated realizes his connection with the whole and look with awareness as the eye of his heart opened, he can easily make sense of his place and his duty in the wholeness and he understands the reasons of his experiences.

The holographic design that enables the human mind to reach the Cosmic Consciousness through its new inspiring knowledge and new energies, answers many ancient questions. It is transforming what has been perceived in thousands year old beliefs and teachings as science-fiction into reality. In your adventure of higher dimension where faith is renewed with science, are you ready to contribute excitement, knowledge and positive influences to the rest of the world with your insights and foresights about the past and the future?

I am ready, let it begin!

Heaven: *You didn't ask, but let me add that when you solve something in the past, you will enlighten something in the future and vice versa; you will enlighten something in the past when you do it for the future. Briefly, there is symmetry in time and you will approach the beginning so much as you advance in future. I need to warn you here: the reality of the known world will change forever along with your perception of reality as you learn about the life forms of the illusionary reality. Each answer will unfold the reasons behind veil of mystery and take you to a very different past as well as a very different future. As the new knowledge increases your expectations and your questions, you will have a difficult time to live with fresh new questions that will really challenge you especially in the beginning.*

'Plato's Cave'

'Let's think of an underground cave: there is an entrance at the front, open to light from end to end whereas there are people who cannot move or turn their heads since they are enchained and they sit with their backs facing the entrance. Let's say there is a fire burning above, behind them. There is a low wall along the way, between the fire and the people whose backs are facing it. And there are some other people behind this wall. And they have some puppets and some tools in their hands made of stone and wood. The ones in the cave cannot turn their heads since they are enchained and they cannot see the others who are outside. What they see are the shadows on the wall across them by the help of the fire.

They think they define the real objects by the names they give to these shadows and that this sound reaching their ears comes from the shadows. If one of them gets unchained and taken out, his eyes will be dazzled by the daylight. He will think that what he saw before was more real. His eyes should get used to the light for him to see the objects.

Such a man will first see the shadows, later the reflections of people and objects on the water and then the objects, the stars, the moon and the sky themselves. When he understands that it's the sun that creates the seasons, the years and it's the sun that arranges the visible world and that the original source of everything seen by the people in the cave is the sun, he feels a pity for them. He looks down on the value they give one another and their thoughts on the shadows in front of them. And they wouldn't believe his word if he goes near his old friends and tell them about what he saw outside. He gets attacked if he attempts to save them or raise them up mentally.

If this allegory is adapted to our subject and we call the cave as 'the visible world', the fire which illuminated the cave as 'the light of the sun that shines on earth' and the beauties watched above as 'the soul rising to the world of ideas', then our idea might be easier to understand.

*You are at the **threshold of the higher dimension** where the things that have been called as science-fiction for thousands of years turn into reality. You are on the **line between knowledge and reality** where the gates of future are opened part way. You have two choices; (1) you may return right away, wake up in your bed and spend the rest of your life talking about a big part of this training you had until now, as an entertaining dream that would attract everyone's attention. You will be brought once you are ready again and we shall continue with the higher dimension training. (2) the knowledge and the experiences that challenge your understanding of reality may enable you to approach to the closest point to the solution of the system and you may begin to share what faith is with those in the world, just as you demanded. Remember; 'what is important is not solving the system but enduring after you solve it.'*

DUALITY IS OVER, GLORY BE TO TRIALITY

Before I say yes to you, I ask you: am I in a dream that was created by my imagination or are you really going to teach me something that I don't know? Can you prove me that you are coming from the higher dimension by showing me something that I don't know, something from your higher dimension so that I can understand the situation and do not get hopeful in vain?

__Heaven:__ Aren't you already satisfied by what you saw and experienced in Dreammatic?

What I saw seems like a dream that a software developer could have seen combining his partial knowledge about virtual reality with his little knowledge of heaven. The higher dimension should include new knowledge, new definitions, new names. It should make me experience a sense of new excitement by bringing in new questions as well as answers that oblige me to make some serious changes on my perspective on life I had in the old dimension.

I can say 'Yes, I am with you forever' only if you show me something that will help me with my holistic improvement and change not only my view point of my own life but also my viewpoint of the universe completely.

__Heaven:__ Actually this question you ask is an evidence in itself that you are not in a dream and we are real. What do you think of the duality which is accepted as the basic structure of the present world?

It is the classical logic system based on two truth values; 1 for true and 0 for false. It is a general term which represents the principles of complementariness and opposition in nature such as 'opposition', 'duality', 'dilemma', 'duplication', 'binary equilibrium', good and evil. It is assumed that everything in the universe has this structure.

Positive	Negative
Plus	Minus
Electron	Proton
Matter	Anti Matter
Spirit	Body
Hot	Cold
Big	Small
Wrong Decision	Right Decision

Heaven: *The duality which is expressed as perfect trueness and wrongness presents two choices as total acceptance and total rejection. Having accepted the matter as absolutely real, is not interested in the process at all. Focusing only on the results, it doesn't take the infinite amount of numbers into consideration between 0 and 1. How could the duality which has two poles and two dimensions explain the 3-D universe which provides limitless choices? There is a triple structure in universe* **called TRIALITY and the duality becomes ONE***.*

Positive	**Neutral**	Negative
Plus	**Zero**	Minus
Electron	**Neutron**	Proton
Matter	**Space**	Antimatter
Spirit	**Human**	Body
Hot	**Warm**	Cold
Big	**Middle**	Small
Wrong Decision	**Indecisive**	Right Decision

When Sinus curve is observed through a 2 dimensional dualistic approach, the dual structure of +/- is seen. When approached with a trialistic view, you begin to see the triplet structure by considering the neutral values on the points of 0°, 180°, 360°. Disregarding these points would be ignoring the neutron in an atom which is composed of electron, proton and neutron. In ancient Egypt, it is said: 'The deities are those who transformed duality into oneness whereas the humans are child deities yet, experiencing the duality in order to know the oneness.'

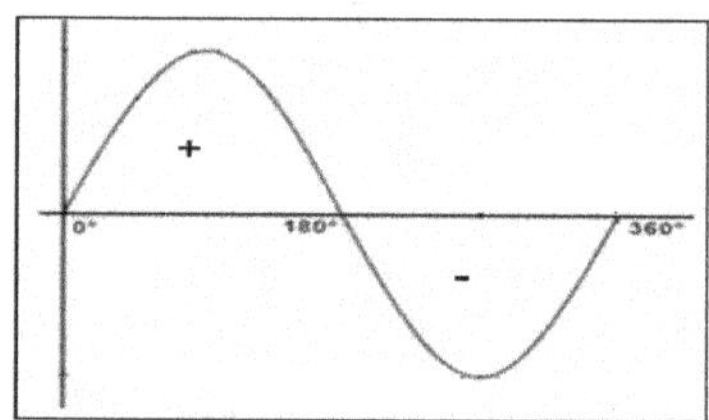

Heaven: *The expression 'let us assume' used by quantum mechanics and the philosophers is an amazing approach which gives a chance for something that hasn't happened to try its possibility to happen.* **The foundation of Quantum reality called fuzzy logic** *that is developed to transcend the inadequacies of the strict and assertive conclusions of classical logic which are unadoptable for life, considers the infinite possibilities between 1 and 0. It confronts the statements which take 1 and 0 as the ultimate right and wrong. Let me illustrate it with a joke of Nasreddin Hodja.*

One day Hodja has two guests. They say: 'We have a disagreement.' One of them tells about his problem and Hodja says 'You are right.'
The other goes ahead and tells about his problem and Hodja says 'You are right' to him as well.

His wife who serves the tea for the guest interrupts them 'What a nonsense this is Hodja, you say both of them are right'. Hodja, after stopping and thinking for a moment, turns to his wife and says 'What can I do, you are also right.'

Just like in this joke, the notion of absolute right and wrong in classical logic created inconsistency in practice. Physics has reached its macro and micro limits regarding the knowledge about living beings.   The answers given by classical physics cannot come up with credible interpretations regarding the movements of matter.   The classical polar logic of duality had inflexibilities which aren't compatible with making decisions in the course of daily life.

The machines were obliged to give more complex answers as their skills developed. This is the point when fuzzy logic comes into the stage, which has a logic structure relatively closer to humans and the language. When it was understood that the matter may show different types of correctness at the same time depending on the observer and that it was determined by the observer's level of knowledge, the ideas of classical physics regarding the daily life were replaced by the approaches of physics based on quantum reality.

Yet the fuzzy logic is not the final point human thought can comprehend. You shouldn't think that it's applicable for any situation. Fuzzy logic can be inadequate in those areas where the concept of infinity is used. There is a very special logic based on intuition to deal with the concept of infinity. But we don't tackle with these in this section.

Everything but you takes shape according to your existence. Only the human has the faculty of choice and he does not have an active interaction with those around him, animate or inanimate, unless he makes a contact with them. They all perform their standard codified processes. Once you get in contact with any of them, it would leave its standard nature since it will be exposed to your influences.

<u>Example:</u> It is an intervention to the nature of flower when you water or prune the flower or even when you talk to it. This action will bind you to a shared future with the flower. What's the matter with you? Are you brooding on how you can explain all these to others in the world?

THE STATE OF KNOWLEDGE THAT IS
FREE FROM TIME OR SPACE

I am brooding on how I can go and live in the world again after all that I learnt. I am ready to change my understanding of trying to comprehend the 3-D universe through a two-dimensional classical viewpoint and receive the 3-D structured new and enlightening knowledge of Triality. Let's begin...

Heaven: Before starting, we need to prepare you for the learning process by clearing away the mental blockages that were formed as the results of your past experiences including the ones from your birth. They would hinder your ability to understand the new knowledge. I need to warn you again; what is being solved loses its meaning.

While understanding brings peace, knowing might bring unsettlement. In your journey to the mystical knowledge, you may experience some serious time distortions due to your changed perception, losses of consciousness (disintegration), lapses of reality or changes in your body image (loss of character). Nothing will be the same for you when you complete the basic training of transition to higher dimension and turn back to the world.

As being someone who has lived both here and in the world dimension and remembers the two, you will need help from time to time in this inter-section where you will be staying until you complete your transition. Therefore you shall have an unconditional trust in us, never be skeptical on any account, leave yourself to us and go with the flow. The worries and fears will distract you and hinder your understanding. Just like the suffering and happiness hinder your understanding in the world dimen-

sion... In order for your 'eye of the soul' open and enable you understand the secrets (essential knowledge) that transcends the visible, you have to 'trust unconditionally'. Don't worry, we don't load anyone to an excessive extent that he cannot handle. We have great trust in you, you should trust us as well.

This mystical euphoria turned to a little anxiety; were they all false illusions including my loved ones, the ones who loved me or the places?

Heaven: Don't worry! It is not the end of the world, it's only the end of the world you know. Just like I told you, have trust in us and go with the flow. If you confront with a reality that you have difficulty to accept at this stage when your extraordinary creativity is encouraged, you will be made to wake up in the normal world and feel as if you have just seen a science-fiction movie. Plus, we will also publish a few science news in the newspaper you read or in a TV show that you watch, which will support what you have seen. So you will be ensured to feel happy with such thoughts as 'I can see the future too! I have thought of this before' and digest what you have experienced.

*If it doesn't suffice, it will be provided that you run after some mundane issues through an **Intentional Imbalance** which is an emotional turmoil that will deeply affect you such as a serious business success or failure, an illness experienced by someone in your family, a separation, a union etc. Do you go on or do you quit?*

I beg your pardon but I really need to learn who makes this offer before accepting it. Only then I can answer you question. I should get to know you at least a little bit if I am to trust you unconditionally. Can I learn your name? Do you

believe in God? Guides are usually male, why are you in a female form? (Heaven transformed into various female and male forms just in seconds and then came back to her original form.)

Heaven: As you see, how much can you trust someone who can take any bodily forms in an illusionary setting when she gives information about her sex and identity?

Are you after the knowledge or the source? Didn't the people miss the original message found in the knowledge for thousands of years just because of discussing about the source of the knowledge or who gives it? They never read the knowledge that was there in so many books or had heeded them unnecessarily just because of the identity of the revealer.

That's why my name is Heaven, because there is not someone else in your life called Heaven. If I say you another name that you know, you will at once compare me with the women who has the same name and create a bias about me from what you have in your subconsciousness about the experiences you had with them. You will recall the things you experienced with her while talking to me. A single gesture or a simple stress in my voice can easily distract you by triggering your emotional intelligence and evoking your memories. A scientific training will not serve its purpose because of emotional blockages.

In case I give knowledge about the countries or belief systems then you will have the same kind of biases for the groups this time. The more you categorize the outer world and other people as 'earthling-alien, believer- non-believer, man-woman, those who are on my side and those who aren't', the more you will be divided in intellect and you will occupied with untimely and un-necessary questions.

If I say I am Muslim to gain some confidence from you, you will go on to ask my sect and then my religious order. If I refer to a verse of Quran or a saying of prophet Mohammad, this time we will be discussing on its meaning while we defend different views on them and we will move off the subject.

The unifying model is not a reference that uses all the sources separately but one that enables different parts reconcile and al-most dissolve in one another while the model itself is not in need of any of them. If you gather a group of people around a table and have their group names written in front of them for the sake of 'unifying people', you will only bring them together, not unify. And they will usually fight for increasing their rights and their share in the whole, rather than fighting for the rights of the whole. Those who are excessively dependant on the only piece in their hands are unaware of the whole because of being unable to see it. The whole, in their eyes, is a scattered whole consisting of uncombined parts rather than a complete whole.

Do you notice that even my gender made your mind quite busy. Why am I in a female form? How would you solve a puzzle which belongs to both spiritual and material dimensions, with-out using both sides of your brain? I am the emotional and intui-tive side of your spirit; it's more important to understand who you are, not who we are. After all, we exist for you to under-stand who you…

What's real must surely be different than a perception but how can I understand the difference between the two? How can I understand that it's illusion here?

***Heaven:** The illusionary happinesses are the false happinesses whose realities are lost as being questioned. And it is a serious stage of courage and a phase of overcoming the mundane ego to question its reality while you can still choose to enjoy it. You wanted four houris in your mansion by the seaside and they came. Would they come if you wanted 40, 100 or even 1000 ones?*

Yes they would.

***Heaven:** Well, where do they come from, who do they belong to? Is it that we have a 'girl farm' consisting of a thousand of virgins and they wait to present themselves to you?*

They are digital, or illusionary houris so to speak, that were created by the matching sensory signals sent to the centers of perception in my brain. They do not exist in reality, they can't belong to anyone.

***Heaven:** You can understand whether what you perceive is illusion or not only when you wake up, because you your brain accepts each perceptive signal it receives as real, not being interested in the source of the signal at all. Shortly, it is quite hard to understand and trust!*

It is not just you; but how can I trust anything that I touch, see or perceive any more? Not only will I be unable to believe in the reality of the world but also I won't be able to decide if illusion is illusion. I will be able to prove neither its reality aspect nor its illusion aspect. All of my reality recognitions and my most basic happinesses are about to end while I am losing my starting point.

*Heaven: This is exactly **the state where the knowledge is in its purest form**, unbounded by time and space. It is the stage where the essential knowledge in the matter is attained while the spirit and matter are disconnected; the stage where time and space lose their reality and importance and knowledge is the only thing being discussed. It is the period when mundane happinesses come to an end and the new energies of the new dimension are felt along with the experience of a new happiness. My advice to you is not to mind them at all as if they are all illusion and to be careful as if they are all real.*

Is it possible for a soul to be happy with knowledge when it got used to get happy with the matter and its reality before? Does the matter set a hindrance in reaching the essential knowledge? Doesn't the part represent the whole?

Heaven: Think of a piece in a puzzle. You can only find out that it is made of cardboard and a colorful material etc if you look at the piece in your hand. The parts may give some hints as to what the whole is made of. Nevertheless in the case of a mental puzzle, you need to bring together a certain number of the critical puzzle pieces that would evoke the wholeness of the picture. If you are in a setting where each piece is a part of the whole, then you are either in a dream or in an illusion in some virtual reality of computers. Actually both are illusions. As being a computer programmer, you are one of those who would learn it in the quickest way and adapt to it. Now it's time to understand what you learnt and put them into practice.

The puzzlement I had was over and I was filled with the excitement to feel that I was on the verge of learning the essential knowledge that would provide me with an extraordinary understanding. I didn't want to feel this remorse I had when I left Dreammatic. With my nature being ever so eager to run after and chase the knowledge, I said 'I want to continue. I am ready, let it begin.' Heaven smiled and said: '*Here is my brave man with his sharp thoughts, determined questions and satisfying answers.*'(Heaven really knows how to pump you up... ☺)

Heaven: Some give the instruction 'never mind if you see something about technology, just disregard it' by saying 'I was never interested in technology, I don't understand anything about it.' So the brain takes these instructions serious and put blockages for those subjects about technology. After that, it listens to the technological topics but doesn't take them serious and never show effort to learn about them. It is just like a camera that doesn't record eventhough it is on.

*Think of your brain as a type of Dreammatic which is doing the things for which you say **LET THERE BE** and not doing those for which you say **LET THERE NOT BE**. People put these blockages on their path without being unaware of it, reprogramming their brains and emotions in almost any area such as love, passion or work by what they express with words about them. The gates of learning in your brain should be opened fully before you start the knowledge here.*

What is the most significant blockage that prevents learning?

Heaven: Of course it's arrogance: rejecting and humiliating other sources of knowledge by seeing yourself and your knowledge superior than everyone else's. Those people who have thoughts like 'Why would I go to his seminar or listen to his talk?' 'Let him come to me!', 'If he comes to my seminar, that means he is here to learn which shows that he accepts my superiority. 'suppose that the piece of the puzzle they have is the whole itself. And they exclude other pieces with observational or unproved reasons like claiming that their frequencies or energies are low based on their fabricated recognitions. On the other hand, the greatest aspect of higher knowledge is its ability to embrace all by having integral viewpoints, not to exclude any kind of lower knowledge.

Arrogance, which is the apparent aspect of not having sufficient belief in what you know, is generally the fear of someone who doesn't know what to do in the face another idea. How can those bring together people with different ideas when they can't bring the ideas together in the first place? How will they transform the essential knowledge which is already scattered in different people and places into an arranged knowledge of wholeness?

Get rid your arrogance first and learn it from wherever or whoever the knowledge has. But remember that there is no enlightenment unless there is purification. In the words of the book İlahi Nizam ve Kainat (Divine Order and the Universe): 'You can't go up to the next floor without withdrawing your foot from the lower. Therefore, you need to purify yourself from your old thoughts, ideas and knowledge, and even the people who wear you out.

Can you explain about these people who wear you out a little bit? Isn't everyone around me in the world dimension there for me to recognize myself in them, for evolution in other words? How can I discern the ones that wear me out?

Heaven: *Let me first tell you about the ones who renew you and then you will understand who the others are. They are those people who inspire you, people who are at peace with themselves and with their surrounding. They are not necessarily people of science or people from higher positions. They are the people who live an ordinary life without being ordinary. They honor the humanity through their courage, their honor and hardworking character they have. We don't talk about the others in order not to publicize them.*

Everything is your choice. Do not exclude anyone but be very careful with those whom you want to include in your immediate surrounding to share your privacy. Let me illustrate it with an anecdote.

TWO SYMBOLS

The wise old Native American tribal chief was watching the two wolf dogs who struggle with one another, sitting in front of his hut with his grandchild. One of the dogs was white while the other was black. And those dogs ever fought with each other in front of his grandfather's hut as the child recalls. Those were the dogs that his grandfather always kept near. The child always thought one would be enough to protect the hut and now he decides to understand why his grandfather needed another one and specifically a white and a black one. He asked, curious to know:

The old wise Chief patted the child on the back and said: 'They are two symbols for me.'

'What do they symbolize?' asked the child.

'The symbols of good and evil. The good and evil in us constantly struggle just like those dogs. Watching them has always made me contemplate on this. That's why I always keep them with me.'

And the child thought: 'There should be a winner if there's a fight.' and went on with another one of those never-ending questions that every child loved to ask. 'Well, who do you think will be the winner?'

The wise man looked at his son with a deep smile and said: 'Which one? ***The one I feed most!'***

As you see, you decide which one to feed with those who are in your immediate surrounding.

This reminds me of this scene in 'Lord of the Rings' where the evil men find out where the child is when he puts on the ring. You active the energy of anything as you talk about it and they surround you at once, trying to get you. Just like this old saying: 'Prepare the stick as you mention the dog.'

Heaven: *You got what you needed to understand. Just repeat after me now!*

I gave the instruction that will lift all my blockages. 'Let all the blockages be lifted that come from my birth and my past, that hinder my ability to understand the Holographic Dimension's trainings about virtual reality and advanced technology for the good of all. I am ready to change all I know with better ones!' I started to wait, all my learning channels being open.

Heaven: The mankind who has been observing the universe that has superhuman greatness and a superhuman variety, have those assumptions:

(1) 'It couldn't be I and a group of people who made the universe, he who made it should be superhuman.'

(2) 'Anything that I can touch, that I can see with my eyes and hear with my ears, briefly anything I perceive is real.'

These assumptions are the traditional acknowledgments of the perception-based world. And it's quite a peaceful time for the mankind in which he feels himself secure through believing that he didn't create this universe whose reality he never doubts about. The opposite would cause an old and deep consciousness turn into suspicion. We call this state as 'reality lapse' which feels like a real chaos for many people. How would you define the location of what you know in the wholeness?

"GNOTHİ SEAUTON!" KNOW THYSELF! BUT HOW?

What I already know is not even a dot compared to what I should know. It is almost like a drop in the ocean.

Heaven: Why did you describe it that way?

That's how scientists and philosophers have defined it for thousands of years. Isn't it? What else do we know?

Heaven: This is a great example for the social **blockage.** *In the first eras when there was no knowledge at all, the man who felt weak in the face of the things he saw, defined himself as 'a drop in the ocean' inspired by the physical area the earth covered in space. And those who intended to attain the knowledge for how the universe started, which is a divine puzzle, make such a comment: 'what we know* **is not even a dot compared to what we should know. It is almost ZERO.** *So what is it that you should know?*

I don't know.

Heaven: Alright. How can you determine anything about the ra-tio between what you should know and what you already know, without ever knowing what it is that you should know? And why do you accept it to be zero? (x/? = 0) And where will this ac-ceptance lead you?

Considering that it is impossible to answer this question, focus on the world and the mundane things instead of searching for the answer. You try to get stronger in where you are if there is no other place to go.

Heaven: The questions that have been asked for thousands of years are; 'where did we come from?' and 'why did we come from?'. Mankind has spent thousands of years for these unan-swered questions using lacking information and creating an-swers. They even adapted the questions to themselves to create answers **desperate of trying to prove something that cannot be proved.** *While they say 'Stop asking these unanswered ques-tions which do not help anyone in anyway', they themselves have created hundreds, thousands of so-called answers that 'seemed like answers' based on assumptions that consisted of nothing but hopes, dreams and the darkest nightmares. The causality principle that claims 'if this exists, there has to be something which created it.' has been the most accepted an-swer of all. Here is a great anecdote to explain how it does not take us anywhere:*

'One day, a well-known scientist (Bertrand Russell as rumor has it) was giving a speech on astronomy. He explained how the

earth revolved around the sun and the vast star cluster called galaxy. At the end of his speech, a small old woman stood up and said: 'Everything you have just said is nonsense. The earth rests on the back of a tortoise.' And the scientist answered with a vibrant smile on his face : 'So what does this tortoise stand on?'

'You are bright my lad, very bright.' said the old lady. 'But it is all tortoises underneath!'

Let's leave aside these questions of 'Where did we come from' and 'why did we come?' that seek the beginning and which are asked quite untimely because of the lacking knowledge. We should ask new questions about the future instead of the past, by turning our attention to our close future using the existing knowledge, technology and intuition. Just as they say **'the teacher appears when the student is ready'; 'the answer appears clearly once the right question is asked.'**

If you can't find answers to these questions that have been asked over thousands of years, then you should begin to ask new questions that transcend the traditional assumptions like Copernicus who said: 'I cant solve the celestial phenomena when I base them on the belief that the stars revolve around our earth. So I will try the opposite. I will consider the celestial phenomena believing that it 's the earth that revolves around them. In short, they should be new questions asked for new answers. When you start to ask **'What is it that I am living in? What could it be that is hiding behind this secrecy?,** the answers start to appear and you begin to move to the next higher dimension.

This reminded me of this advice in Dreammatic *'Do not determine who created it before understanding what it is that you are living in!'*. Was this the perspective we failed to adopt?

Heaven: Definitely. Aristotle's insight 'Nature abhors a vacuum' is valid on a mental level as well. The models of human thought which we can call as details and are produced about these unanswered questions prevent us to reach the essence of the answer and the belief. Whereas a right question is a question that can create totally new conditions from a current one and can accomplish what is said to be unaccomplishable and that can make you solve what is said to be unsolvable. It is a question that brings out the essence of believing without destroying the old approach completely but by opening up a new horizon and eliminating all the unnecessary details from our understanding which was based on lacking knowledge.

(And now we were at the gates of the Apollo Temple in Delphi. Heaven asked me: 'What is written there over the gate?')

Gnothi Seauton!" in Latin. Know Thyself.

Heaven: Now, let's talk about this ancient and crucial advice 'Know Thyself' which is a serious clue that has been turned into 'a nice little saying', remained not understood for hundreds of years. What could have been implied by this saying?

'Find yourself', 'find the purpose of creation, the reason behind your existence', 'find the purpose and the source of life' 'find what's there for you...'

Heaven: Yes, that's almost how it was understood. The mankind was sure of the reality he was living in that he only sought to 'Know Himself' on a mental level by asking 'who am I, why am I here, what's my duty?'. And he was never sure of his answers which he found through his intuition and could not go beyond general assumptions. Whereas the advice 'Know Yourself' was also valid for the physical realm as well. But they did not take notice of the simple working system of the human body and its communication with the whole, while they were looking down on the earthly body that represented the ego.

Knowing yourself included what you consist of, how you perceive and how you decide. in short it included understanding how your body worked. If you solve the working principle of the body, you can solve where the body is working in and understand what body depends on while working. You can even solve the purpose behind its creation. You will understand who and what your are when you understand what it is that you are living in. **'He who knows himself will know his God.'**

But how will I come to know these without knowing all the knowledge in the Collective Memory?

Heaven: If you take 'knowing' as knowing everything in the Collective memory, then your knowledge will indeed be like a drop *compared to what you are able to know in the ocean of knowledge of the Collective Memory. To find the answer, it's enough if you know what you need to know, you don't need the whole knowledge. Just as you don't need to know the ever in-creasing knowledge on the internet. It is enough for you to know the operating and using logic and to use it when needed. What you know is like a tiny dot, almost zero, compared to the knowledge on the internet. but the question is what is internet, how does it work and who made it? You don't need to know all the processes and the technology of production about each piece of the car you drive eventhough you are interested in who produced it and who much it cost.*

The purpose is not to know everything by reading all the books, you don't need to drink the ocean to quench your thirst!

Drematic, Fearmatic, Thinkmatic, you have created a copy almost for everything? What are all these?

Heaven: *let me put it this way: it is more important how heaven influences people, the energy of heaven in other words, rather than what heaven is. It is an energy of hope that motivates people to have positive feelings and become better people, not a place where people come and leave. As you see, we are inspired by God and designed it for humanity. You are going to learn them one by one but lets continue with the limits and secrets first.*

The environment just changed in a second and we were again in my luxurious mansion in this place where the forest merges with the sea. Heaven: **'Don't you think something is missing?**

I was in a little attention test. I observed my environment attentively: the forest, the sea, personnel, harem, the boat crew and the tropical wind. Everything seemed in its place. Heaven, realizing that she wouldn't get an answer, said 'isn't it too silent for a forest?

But didn't I just wish for everything that was supposed to be there when I said 'forest'?

Heaven: *You wished for a house with a personnel, a boat with a crew but you didn't specify any details about what's in the forest or the sea. You only said forest. Which animal s should be in it?*

You didn't specify any animals like birds, lions or tigers. What will be in the sea? Dolphins, sharks?

I guess I won't have the chance to enjoy because of dealing with all those details. Specifying the content is something else that brings stress. Did I come to Dreammatic to worry if something is missing or not, or to enjoy myself?

Heaven: *It is so hard to find an easy person. People would like every wish they make come true but they also ask if it will be them to think of the details. ☺ how will the details be known in a setting where everything is as you wish, if you don't specify them? You should think that Dreammatic is the smartest fool on earth. You need to define everything just as in the case of* *computers. Your wish will manifest in a general way and Dreammatic will complete the details or leave their place emp-ty when you don't give any details.*

It Would have been quite nice to have a Dreammatic that showed sympathy! So why didn't it fill up my forest by com-pleting it?

Heaven: *Because you didn't give it full authorization.*

Looking up, I said: **'Dear Dreammatic, as you very well know what I like and dislike, you can fill in the empty places in a way that will benefit me. I trust you.'** (as I said this, it looked like a real forest with the birds and the bugs singing, and with squir-rels and gazelles wandering around. This is what they call natu-ral meditation.) **How many groups of people are there in Dreammatic?**

DREAMMATİC, THINKMATIC and THE BASIC CRITERIA

Generally, there is a (1) a group of people who desire to change their environment who dream of houses, cars, boats, jewelry, a boy friend/ girlfriend. (2) a group of people who want to change something about their personality or physical body; those who say they would like to be taller, to have bigger breasts, tight hips, blue eyes, who would like to be like a model, strong like Hercules, an important person, or would like to have a good po-sition. In short, what a person lacks in the World or Thinkmatic are the first things he wants in Dreammatic.

One has to feel that he is totally by himself and should not be conscious like me, in order to be happy and comfortable in Dreammatic. How can someone become happy in his dreams if he knows that he is constantly spied on by you? On the other hand, how will someone who has his memory erased experience his first moment in Dreammatic? No communication and no memory. How do you teach such a person to direct Dreammatic?

Heaven: Good question. First let us examine the first visit to Dreammatic:

1. <u>The first visit to Dreammatic:</u> It is no different than a newborn baby in the world. A human when he is not conscious is just like a baby who acts through his essential self. He is not even aware of his sex. He cant make sense of anything. Everything for him is something to learn by trying in the beginning and he will only be able to distinguish some basic concepts such happiness/ unhappiness, beneficial/harmful. We have the total control in Dreammatic and people do not know yet that they can shape up their environment. So another person of the opposite sex is sent to him to observe his reactions. Once they are intimate, it is observed if he loves the opposite sex or not, the degree of his love and the his way of love is measured. His sexual aspect begins to evoke and it is provided that he adapts himself to the opposite sex he's together with.

Therefore, after hundreds and thousands of contacts, it is provided that he collects information for comparing and that he has a basic concept of beauty and happiness. Just as stated in the book İlahi Nizam ve Kainat (The Divine Order and The Uni-

verse), 'After this point, some new and more sophisticated needs start to evoke in his soul. The soul, having new types of needs, starts to expect more meaningful reactions from the contacts he physically makes with the opposite sex and his surrounding in a wider scope. These new type of needs directly reflect on the body and his respond is received through his body. So the being who serves his soul, causes to happen some necessary events in relation to these new type of needs, through influencing the heavy matter and the other bodies around him.'

Then comes the second stage. Now the soul who was adapted to happiness is made to experience lacking and he is not given what he wants. His reactions in relation to lacking (addiction, crying, complaining) and what he will do in his first encounter after the lacking period are all measured. It is also observed, measured and graded what he might do to the opposite sex when he is not given what he wants (observing if he is inclined to violence). All tests and the basic needs of human are included in one of these:

1. **Hunger / Fullness**
2. **Self-Protection (Reflexive)**
3. **Sex**

The character simulation which emerges as the result of the measurement and individual testing of nutrition, sex, other things that give pleasure etc that we call physical drives make up the criteria to begin in Thinkmatic.

2.Later visits to Dreammatic: *think of it this way, what makes others happy? A place that someone longs for is like a heaven for him. a heaven is a warm place For a person who lives up in the north, while it is a safe forest for someone who has to live and raise his child amongst wild animals, snakes and poisonous insects in a rainforest. For someone who lived thirstiness throughout his life and who long s for the green, a forest filled with trees and rivers can be a starting scene that will fascinate him. Usually, a certain part at the stage is planned as a desert for a graduated transition. A person feels safe in the places that are known to him. He feels himself happy and peaceful but he doesn't remember why. Because his memory about the past is covered in Dreammatic. You might ask if these are important for someone who doesn't 'remember about his past. A man without a memory would like anything he is given.*

Erasing the memory of someone doesn't mean erasing his sub-consciousness and intuition which we call the essential con-sciousness. His karmic aspects or his intuitive karma like the bi-ases, emotions etc he has gained in his childhood remain as they are.

As The person goes beyond his bodily thirst and the physical ex-citements, as he overcomes his fear of losing and begins to con-trol the time and space, Dreammatic start to adapt itself to him. The scenes which reflect the subconsicousness of the individuals begin to shape one by one through mutual adaptations. They don't have to say 'LET THERE BE' as you do, it just happens when they think.

You are in direct contact with us in a conscious state because you are not here to live in Dreammatic. you are here to receive a training in understanding its limits and the logic behind it.

I continue with my questions as an inquisitive student. Do you stay forever in Dreammatic? In what order do you experience them; first the Thinkmatic and later Dreammatic?

Heaven: How would you define eternal LOVE?

It is the LOVE that will never end, experienced by the lovers who never think about separating in whatsoever circumstance. They have no trust issues and never abandon one another neither on earth nor in the afterlife. They are those who give their word in their promise of marriage not as 'until death' which describes love in this world but by claiming that instead of houris/ male companions in heaven, they want each other in heaven as well: 'To all those visible and invisible, …. İs my woman/ man both in this world and afterlife. ….'

Heaven: The eternity you sense here is what you feel when you don't have any fear of losing and when you suppose that something will never end. If you don't become one with the person you have an intercourse, you are only mating, discharging yourself in other words. Whereas when you hug and smell your beloved with an intention to unite with her, you realize that you experience Divine Love while you feel that you are approaching God in the endless ocean of love in the Dimension of Truth. You experience love, as if you are in an eternal dream.

About the order, you first go into Dreammatic and then Thinkmatic.

After Thinkmatic, there is the eternal Dreammatic again.

It creates a sense of eternity in people when they don't have any fears of losing or concerns as to something will decrease or finish in Dreammatic. Why would someone stay in Dreammatic eternally? An eternity spent here unconsciously would do no good for us or the person himself. We use Dreammatic to determine the starting criteria of Thinkmatic.

Am I in the world, in Thinkmatic or Dreammatic? Well actually it doesn't matter which. Both are chains of intertwined structures composed of peculiar and secret events.

THE CENTRAL MIND and THE FALSE APOCALYPSE

Heaven: Beware not to go in the same circle because of the same rashness! You promised that you would trust in the beginning, please allow the training unfold in its own pace. Do not tire me or yourself, just focus on here for now. Do not try to jump to some other topics whose turns have to wait for now. How will you understand the lessons in the future without understanding these? Will you be one of those people who have ideas while lacking in knowledge? We talked about 'total surrender and unconditional trust. Unconditional trust is total surrender. It is also a form of unconditional surrender and an unconditional trust as well to say 'Things have a way of turning out for the best!'.

Does not the complete surrender hinder questioning?

Heaven: Surrendering is trusting without having enough information. As you see, the purpose of total surrender here is to focus on the knowledge instead of the teacher, unite with the knowledge and reach the mystery behind it. If you are confused, the unification cannot be completed because the eye of your heart has nor been opened yet. The mankind is usually result-oriented, he is impatient and rash. He want to go the final point at once. If his success criterion is finishing the journey, he will miss many things he should see and understand because of his questions such as 'Did we arrive?' or ' When are we going to arrive there?'. It is true for the games as well. Humans are usually interested in the result of the game and being a winner. Whereas the Creator evaluates how you play and how much effort you show. He assesses how you lose or win it, rather than just seeing over if you win or not. and you should be a little patient to understand if you win or not.

If you evaluate people according to the results they have, not knowing or caring about their stories then that means you only see them as machines or robots consisting of numbers and results. This is no different than undervaluing the people in Thinkmatic or Dreammatic and seeing them only as digital puppets. If your environment is your reflection, then they exist only for you. Those who exist only for you, cannot have a will of theirs since they will be acting according to you. All of them are illusions created for you by the Central Mind that controls them with you. Many do not see that the digital puppets are only reflections of the Central Mind and keep fighting with the shadows because of showing too much interest in them. It is just like the case of bulls who focus on the red fabric, being a victim of their instincts and cannot see the matador. There are also exceptions of course.

Is that why Yunus Emre said 'I tolerated the created, because of the Creator.'?

Heaven: The love Yunus experienced was one of the hardest of all tests of love: Love of Truth. Yunus did not interfere with the matter and has been one of those who attained the highest level of patience through enduring the sufferings required by the unconditional trust and surrender. Being in that stage where there were no mysteries left, he devoted himself to holistic service when he saw that all he has gone through was for the whole. So he took his place in history as an example for all the mankind. Service to God can be achieved through serving to what He created. Serving the community is serving God. Total surrender is 'not being sadder or happier' than needed.

Am I at this point about which they say 'do not think about it much or you will lose your mind!'? Was I raw, cooked and then burnt?

Heaven: We are not at these difficult sections yet. You need to complete the levels of knowledge, experience and intuition in this current dimension. What challenge people are not the unanswered questions but the new answers and the new questions brought up by these answers. 'It is not important to solve the system but to endure after you solve it.'

Well I was expecting some things more visible than that, like some giant computer centers or interesting devices when you talked about superhuman technological design. You said:

**'Sometimes making something visible might destroy the faith.'
Is that why you don't show the system room?**

Heaven: The system rooms are still there but do you think that the mystery will end when you go beyond this secrecy and see them? Was the mystery completely solved when the mysteries of the fire, cow, moon and sun gods were solved? Are you sure you are living in the world that was created by God? Technology becomes ever more sophisticated and mysterious when it can erase and control human memory and human thought.

Many think that transition to a higher dimension is a classical apocalypse scenario where the world will be destroyed. There is another group of those who believe that they will continue with their lives in the space after being taken by a starship. How will I understand that I am in an higher dimension?

Heaven: They are not seekers, they are the ones who wait. They wait for the space ship version of Noah's Ark. Just like in the example of tortoise, these are all foresights that can only take us one step further bur cant not answer the questions like what will happen there or how long they will be staying there. what will happen them when a certain number of people are taken to a spaceship? Will the aliens feed them forever? Will they release

them to another planet similar to the world? Going away has always been an attractive choice for humans. This is just a sacred scenario of salvation that includes only a group for those who are tired of this world and the problems they live, having no hope for changing their lives.

There is the condition of 'Beneficialness for the Whole' in everything God wants from the people. A plan which doesn't give importance to some parts in the whole and does not include all is not a plan coming from the wholeness. Because it doesn't fulfill God's condition of Beneficialness for the Whole'. Be very careful with this detail, just as the Mayans have told: 'Do not let even one person to stay behind.' As you see, wrong expectations hinder the ability to see with awareness. Those who expect a physical transition, cannot realize the mental transition for a long time.

So how will I understand that the current dimension has come to an end?

Heaven: how would you define a dimension?

I would say 'the current universe I live in'

Heaven: how would you specify its boundaries?

From earth to the end of the space.

Heaven: Isn't the higher dimension out of the space and isn't the space infinite?

Yes. When I think of space as a superhuman mysterious structure, I think the higher dimension should be beyond this mystery.

Heaven: If space is a superhuman hindrance that the human is unable to overcome, who will you reach the higher dimension beyond the mystery without transcending the space?

It seems like there is no other chance than using the evidences which are believed to be coming from the higher dimension. We tend to think that they will be coming to us if it's not possible for us to go there. There are even those think that the dimension of the world should be completely destroyed before God should make Himself visible to us. If those who pass away go to the higher dimension, we will all go to a higher dimension collectively when the world is destroyed.

Heaven: So you say that it's a collective escape of those who want to get rid of the conditions as well as themselves. While there is no substantial scientific evidence as to show that the end of the world is coming; why would someone go after a scenario of a collective destruction based on only some assumptions? Sometimes when you want to change something in your life and it is really something fundamental that seems impossible to change, you oppress that in your subconscious level by accepting its impossibility. No matter how much you suppress it, it will come out in such different ways that you wouldn't even realize. Are those who go after such scenarios of apocalypse the ones who want to take out their secret feelings about being destroyed (suicide) that they suppressed in their subconsciousness and melt these feelings in the waters of the scenarios of suicide ? do they feel a willingness to disappear for the sake of finding something better and being happy in the higher dimension? It would be of much more benefit for the tired and jaded souls if they just looked for some symptoms of happiness instead of omens of apocalypse.

Those who try to prepare humanity for the apocalypse by giving the 'Apocalypse Alarm' supported by the channeling knowledge they have much confidence in, create much harm to their own souls with every apocalypse that doesn't take place. As far as I understand, those who say there will be a transition to the higher dimension might get wrong in the method while they know about the transition.

Heaven: you are right, it is about interpreting the clues regarding the transition in a different way. Nothing happens instantly in the universe, everything takes a process. Those who interpret the process in a wrong way and expect a transition through a physical destruction cannot save themselves from the sudden shock they experience when they see that the limits of the knowledge of a higher dimension have been overcome. If you believe in coincidences in your life, that means you cannot observe your life carefully and cannot read the messages of your life.

What do you think of the Mayan Calendar?

Heaven: Calendar is a method to divide the time in years, months and days. The end of a calendar means a beginning of another era. According to the Mayan Calendar; the period that starts after the calendar comes to an end, is what they call the sixth world or 'between the two worlds', 'the transition between the worlds', 'the cycle when the darkness and light unite' or 'the age of transition'. the ancient Mayans, believed that the time of the sixth world point to the beginning of a new Age in which the truth is revealed. Let's see which age or dimension is going to take place... ☺

I couldn't make the connection between changing dimensions and the beginning of a new age. How could the transition to a higher dimension be? You go there in an instant or you simply don't!

Heaven: *A dimension is defined by the restrictions of knowledge and perception that belongs to the reality in which you live in. It has vertical and horizontal stages in itself.*

*There are three stages in a vertical context: **(1)** Earth **(2)** Sky **(3)** Space,*

*And three others in a horizontal context **(1)** Your place of Birth (Family / Neighborhood / City) **(2)** Your country **(3)** The World you live in.*

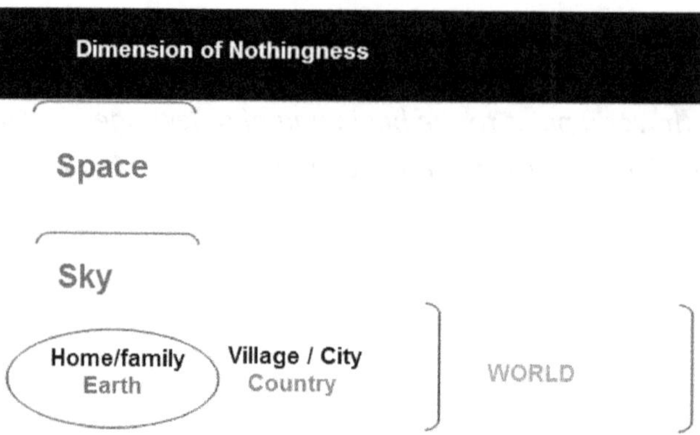

In order for you to go up to the higher or outer dimension, you need to complete the horizontal and vertical phases of your current dimension either physically or mentally. Think about the person who lived millions of years before. His life, his dimension in other words, consisted of his cave on earth and the environment surrounding his cave. Then, he started to go to distant places on earth and he began to discover. so he expanded his dimension horizontally. And he completed the 1st, 2nd and 3rd stages horizontally by almost leaving no single place that he hasn't stepped on earth by using horses, ship and cars.

And later with balloons, airships and planes he conquered first the sky and then the 2.stage atmosphere. He stopped when it came to the 3.stage which seemed to be superhuman. He had journeys with or without human beings to short distances such as the moon, sun and the planet Mars. Yet he accepted the space in which he cant live as something fatal, infinite and impossible to transcend. He tried to discover the space through telescopes, space satellites and infrared vision devices etc and he is still working on it. As the knowledge increased, our dimen-

sion expanse which began on earth, has reached until the end of the space mentally if not physically.

Then ı will be ready to go up to the higher dimension when my limits of knowledge reach the end of the space...

CONSCIOUS AWARENESS and
VERTICAL KNOWLEDGE LEAP

Heaven: *Going to the highest limits of the current dimension does not necessarily mean to go to the other end of the space physically. It is a process that needs to be completed mentally by solving the logic behind its direction and production technology. The transition is a mental one rather than a physical one.*

In which stage do we find peace? Is there peace at all?

Heaven: *Those people who do not know what they seek, experience the unpeacefulness of not knowing what they search for. These souls who have an unpeaceful energy and frequency, should be in their preperation for the transition through the balancing of their spiritual energy and frequency. Instead of encouraging them search for new things and later make them confirm what they found and allowing them to struggle with the reactions, they are given the training of old knowledge which guarantees that they will find peace.*

In this age when Nirvana, which literally means 'reaching quietness' or 'being deflated' is shown as the symptom of finding God, the available knowledge of the common thinking system is used. These teaching make you almost like the well-behaved children. You cant hear new ideas, new energies or surprises neither from the person who gives them nor the ones who receive. They fall asleep while listening with the purpose of awakening and you think it is good for them since they leave the training as rested and calmer. The teachers of this peaceful environment transform these souls that have unpeaceful energies and frequencies into well-behaved children and prepare them so that they are able to receive the knowledge for the transition.

What happens after this peaceful stage?

Heaven: *Those minds whose energies and frequencies are balanced are transferred to the Conscious Awareness stage. This is realized through the knowledge of transition which encourages one to dream of those places that humanity hasn't stepped yet, make fresh starts and experience excitement. This is not a stage where one sings and the others fall asleep, it is the stage where everyone sings, dances while the sprits become one with the wholeness.*

This stage of unification is a period of high energy that changes not only our approach to the concept of the universe but also our life styles and our spiritual journeys. It is a phase where creative minds who search for the new are supported and the minds are enlightened in glow. The enthusiasm of Archimedes, who had the creative intelligence that discovered the buoyancy of water, when he rushed out to the streets naked, shouting 'I have found it!', is a good example to express the high and vigorous energies of the conscious awareness phase. Just as Plutarch stated: 'Human mind is not a bowl to be filled, it is a hearth to be kindled.'

What happens to those who can't go on to the conscious awareness phase?

Heaven: When you suppress your intuitive inner voice, attribute excessive value on some incidents and allow the daily troubles and problems of Thinkmatic take over your mental ego, you will work hard only to acquire material wealth and position and imprison yourself in Thinkmatic.

What is the vertical knowledge leap?

Heaven: You should receive the necessary knowledge of transition that will provide you with the foresight which will open up new horizons about the future by transcending the current limits. This knowledge will also help you understand the course of events and what they are in reality. The Love for Truth is the love you feel to know the Truth. And Knowing the Truth requires the Knowledge of Truth.

Heaven: Remember that you asked 'Am I in heaven?' and then 'Am I in the Heaven of God' and later 'Am I in a fake Heaven?' as you saw whatever you wished for was taking place. You first asked using your worldly knowledge and then through your knowledge of illusion. What determined your questions was the level of your knowledge.

There is a threshold knowledge in each training and everything progresses quite with difficulty until you come to this threshold. When you make the vertical knowledge leap by transcending the threshold knowledge, that means you have learnt the fun-

damental principles and the philosophy of this dimension. So the period of conscious awareness begins for you.

You say that the mankind who made the evolutionary leap in his body, could not make the mental leap or the knowledge leap. Why is knowledge so important, can't we reach the higher dimension through intuition?

许立荣董事长会见美国兼总裁

Heaven: Do you speak Chinese?

No!

Heaven: alright. Can you find a Chinese book by yourself without getting any help if I take you to a library in China?

Of course not.

Heaven: You see, you wouldn't know what to do here or make any sense of it if you didn't have the fundamental technical knowledge. So you would not be able to go beyond those statements originating from some nice feelings you experienced through your body such as 'I get goose bumps, I am in tears, I felt the pure love in my cells, this is an incredible experience'

You would feel that you are not alone and you are a part of something bigger but you would not understand what it is that you are a part of. As you see here, such nice feelings can simply be attained by stimulating the related parts in the brain.

If you experience bewilderment, that means you don't have knowledge, you only have the feeling. If you have knowledge, you will be amazed with admiration to see with your conscious awareness that something you know is being transformed into reality.

THE GURU KNOWLEDGE and THE GOLDEN AGE OF KNOWLEDGE

Briefly what you are saying is 'we can't understand with limited knowledge'! but the technical knowledge should depend on formulas, definitions and assumptions as well. The concepts should come to a point where everyone understands them.

Heaven: That is very true. Because the knowledge is insufficient by itself. Everyone looking at the same scientific results and nature does not necessarily see the same thing. Awareness or what's evoked in the depths of your soul is more important than anything else. Something in your essence gets activated sometimes when you see a thing. It allows you to realize that thing in yourself and see that you always had it concealed in you. When you look at a scientific knowledge or event that's ordinary for everyone, you see the essential knowledge there and you remember. This knowledge which activates and reveals something in you is called the **Guru Knowledge.**

Through his actions, the Guru inspires the student by using examples and scenes that do not require technical knowledge and reminds him what's already in his nature. And the student whose perceptive faculties are enhanced now, should contribute something new to this enhancement and make us of it by learning useful knowledge.

By the way, you shouldn't identify the guru only with people. Nature, the laws of nature, animals, science and technology are all gurus that evoke something in people. You should go after the knowledge which evokes something in you and makes you meet with yourself. The laws of nature are universal since they are the laws of God and they do not belong to any group. You may have guidance from the laws of nature and scientific data, provided that you use them for the good of all, with the purpose of justice and love.

I understand knowledge but why justice and love?

*Heaven: The universe is founded on justice and love; they provide the foundation for nature. The basic sciences like physics and chemistry are the visible natural laws while justice and love are the invisible ones. Science without justice and love turn into weapons that destroy humanity under the command of arms industry. Science exists for us to unify, share and embrace one another; not for us to kill each other or the other living beings. Mustafa Kemal Atatürk who strived to make his people experience vertical knowledge leaps, aimed to prepare his people to the **Golden Age, Divine Knowledge Age** in other words by helping the people approach the highest levels of knowledge in the current dimension. His words **'The truest guide in life is science'** illustrate his purpose.*

Will there be gold everywhere in the Golden Age? We would emphasize the gold which represents the ego and the matter when we say the Golden Age. It is the knowledge that enlightens the human beings, not the gold. So the knowledge should be emphasized, not the matter. It should be called as 'THE GOLDEN AGE OF KNOWLEDGE' to highlight that knowledge is more valuable than the gold.

Heaven: Your words set an example for how the empty spaces or missing parts are completed in Dreammatic. In Dreammatic, sometimes you are given excessively or with short-comings and you are expected to find out about them. Here you were given a missing information and you completed it.

The Golden Age of Knowledge is an age where it is understood that the world we live in is an illusionary life form and that the matter, time and space lose their importance. The gold, which represents the worldly ego loses its value while knowledge and awareness become as valuable as gold has been once. This age, where science pursues the ideas which produce Sophisticated Technologies through foresights about future, is also called the **Divine Knowledge Age** *because of its Divine Technology. The Golden Age of Knowledge leads mankind in experiencing the expected* **Vertical Knowledge Leap** *through the advanced realities. It is the time when the bridges between you and the higher dimension are established.*

How will I understand that I am getting close the Age of Golden Knowledge or the higher dimension. What are the clues?

If you being to struggle with vicious circles dealing with the same problems and keep going to those personal development meetings which lack excitement and whose real purpose is socialization and relaxation then that means the current dimension is over for you intuitively. If you spend aimless and hopeless days going through uninteresting events; you are not living any more, you are just trying to live.

Since transition to a higher dimension is dreamt of as a physical transition, everyone is in a state of waiting. In this period where the reality does not coincide with the prophecies, the unhappiness and the unsettlement increase. Then the answer is sought in fanatically holding on to the old viewpoints which already become unsatisfactory. Stricter rules and punishments are applied in belief systems in order to avoid the collapse within their own systems. In this period when no one shows the effort to understand one another, the only purpose has become to use each other for selfish reasons.

The constriction caused by the collapse triggers the unsettlement, unhappiness and chaos. Intense upheavals are created through making different groups who are of the same faith fight with one another so that they are distracted and their negative energies get discharged. These fanatical groups which cannot improve themselves because of being isolated from the others, start to try oppressing the others using 'group nationalism' and forcing others to adopt their answers and beliefs. These emotional groups who posses a high degree of negative energy, are ready to wait and do anything commanded by their leader as being communities who do not have their own ideas. This wrong expectation can be exemplified with an anecdote:

The Reproach of the Priest

The people were being evacuated in a village which was about to be buried under a dam lake.

While everyone was deserting the village, the priest told them to go and that God would rescue him by sending him a boat. So the villagers didn't insist and left. One day the water went up to the level of the tables in his house and the villagers came to take the priest with a boat. But the priest wouldn't go with them saying that God would rescue him by sending a boat. The villagers left and came again one day later. This time the water has risen to the roof level. The priest, this time on the roof, told them to go away and that God would rescue him by sending him a boat. On the third day the villagers came with an helicopter and the priest who had to go up to the top of the bell tower because of the water, again told the villagers to go away and rejected their help. And the villager found the dead body of the priest when they came again one day later.

Meanwhile the priest was sitting at the corner of the Heaven, sulking, while everyone was enjoying themselves happily. They came and asked in curiosity: God has taken you into His Heaven. Why do you sulk?'. The priest answered: 'I have devoted my life to pray Him for forty years. And there was just one time I really needed something from Him but he didn't take care of me.' At that moment, there was a thunder in the sky. And God said 'You man, I sent you two boats and a helicopter. And you didn't get in. What else could I have done more?'

Unsettlement and unhappiness increase so much in the process of waiting that people are obliged to make a transition to somewhere else. People run after the plans to make the transition to the higher dimension which seek happiness outside and end up in frustration. Wrong expectations in this time when the hopes die, the unrest increases and each plan is proven to be futile, hinder the ability to see the answers. It is not seen that the promised higher dimension is a different perspective of reality developed for the current dimension in the world, rather than being a physical place high up in the sky.

They aren't aware that the higher dimension which they seek to find peace will bring more unsettlement!

THINKMATIC

Heaven: *People always worry when they face new problems but they adapt the situation after a short time. In each step while passing through the illusion world of the higher dimension, you get rid of the fear, hatred, rage, mercy, fake happiness and negative feelings along with illusion of the people. Instead of these feelings, the desire to reach to unknown new life forms that arouse curiosity and fear, comes to the fore. You feel like you are in love, getting rid of your unhappy relationship and starting up a new life in a blank white page. Dimension of reality is a brand new enthusiasm forcing people to think.*

When you realize that you are in a dream, the mountains, rocks, earth, even people lose their meaning. "We wake up before we sleep" instead of "Being dead before we die."

Heaven: Very well. Due to the ever changing intense scenes involving new knowledge, you may not see the transition knowledge which will unite your present and future and give meaning to your experiences along with the things you learn. You may consider this method which is called "cinema therapy" as a holographic hypnosis or dreaming when you are awake. Conscious detaches from reality against strong fiction, sound and vision and feels like it's in the reality of illusion. You may consider this education as an exciting 3D film. We will understand that how much this film has changed your perception of reality and decide if you can pass to the "Thinkmatic" phase.

What is the basic difference between Dreammatic and Thinkmatic?

*Heaven: In fact both of them are mental laboratories which mental experiments with various scenarios are performed. Dreammatic becomes a three dimensional mirror reflecting your inner world by shaping it outside. If we call Dreammatic **"the introverted state of trance"** which will let you live inside your dreams, then Thinkmatic is **"the extravert state of trance."***

Dreammatic is the things that you experience in the scenarios in your inner world hypnosis, Thinkmatic is the things that you experience in the scenarios in the outer world hypnosis. Your personality simulation is taken out of your dreams and thoughts by offering options with the scenarios programmed on the meas-

urable points of your personality. This is a healing and enhancing mental process revealing the points that should be focused by conducting personality analysis along with producing new scenarios based on the found facts. Imagine yourself being trained about your secrets and passing various tests in the Divine Hall of Mirrors.

"Introverted state of trance", "personal experiences in the hypnosis of your inner world"... You talk in riddles. After all, I think that both of them are the soul hunters chasing our souls. As all the scenes take place in speed of light as soon as we imagine them, where and what is the thing called Levh-i Mahfuz (according to Islamic religion the book that everything that has happened in the past and the things that will happen in the future is written), past records, or in your words The Common Memory, what is it like and what is it made of? Where and how are the memories written and how can they be read? Can I see them physically? Please don't say that "It's a technologic thing even ordinary people can understand" or "The answer is inside us" or "We have that knowledge but if reveal it people will go mad." I want to hear the truth even if its harsh. Knowing the truth is better than being ignorant. If you can't explain these things it means that you don't know them either. Somehow one can explain things if he has the knowledge.

Heaven: *(Laughing) It was a wonderful expression for the suppressed and impatient feelings. God bless you! If you remember we said ,the things that you suffer in this world, will become an* *agenda here. What happened to the man who said he is waiting with patience and curiosity? Where is your patience?*

You are right indeed. Let's call it the desire to know. Can a person in love behave normal?

Heaven: You can't understand digital illusion dimension which is called as holographic dimension, with your analog perspective as you can't see and reach the power under illusion effect making you see illusions by dominating your senses.

If there is nowhere to go or there is no exit, then I am in prison. You keep me in mental prison by imprisoning my mind.

Heaven: Mind predominates substance but illusion is so realistic that it's nearly impossible to think that it's not real. As you said, you understand that the place is a prison once you want to get out. When mankind accepted that the space is impassable, they got physically and mentally stuck in the borders of substance in world dimension.

As life in Thinkmatic is a controlled dream, when one realizes that he is dreaming, the dream collapses. Mankind designing and creating the world dimension with the virtual reality technology won't be able to actualize its expected awakening due to the lack of awareness.

Everybody finds holographic dimension, virtual reality technology, common memory and cosmic conscious concepts more acceptable. So far everything looks fine but how can I possibly integrate with a system that I can't perceive with my senses?

IF YOU CONSIDER 'EGO' USING YOUR EGO, YOU CAN'T SEE THE DIVINE KNOWLEDGE

Heaven: *In order to solve the system that can't be comprehended, you have to ask two simple questions:*

1. *WHAT DOES IT DO? If you find out what it does you might develop ideas about those who do it or why they do it.*
2. *HOW DOES IT FUNCTION? If you understand the way it functions you will find out the facts which the function is based on.*

Let's look at the learning and knowledge process of the mankind: Imagine an electronic eye is put on a visually handicapped. Camera of the electronic eye transforms the vision into an electrical signal and sends it to the visual cortex of the brain via optic nerves. The fact that you should pay attention is, solving of the signal which was sent to brain's visual cortex through the eye. As brain isn't interested in signal source, it takes control of the management of the visual cortex with the remote access chip that will be installed in the visual cortex to make you see things that you don't actually see by sending visions that you want to see.

When electrical codes of the perceptive, emotional and mental activities forming inside the brain are solved, all of them have become measurable and meaningful signals. With the solving of brain signalization, how it reached the records in its memory when needed, all the perception system and memory has become duplicable, storable, modifiable, evaluable and manageable.

Good news for the visually handicapped, promising news for others sensually handicapped.

*Heaven: Priorities determine the attention. Those who evaluate scientific developments by giving priority to their desires and see science like treasure hunting, considered this progress as a profitable medical invention to raise people's life quality. However this technological invention was the basis of Dreammatic and Thinkmatic which would lead to a vertical knowledge leap, make people to get closer to the Divine Region and initiate **the Golden Age of Knowledge.** (I am thrilled by the words Divine Region, Divine Knowledge, and Vertical Leap.)*

BLOCKAGE IN THE PERCEPTION BASED SCIENCE

*As I said the process was important, I have to go back to the beginning of the process and mention the **Blockage In the Perception Based Science** blocking mankind's vertical knowledge leap. If you remember, in the past, dentists used to treat all types of dental problems. But today there are many different dental branches and in the future, there will be sub branches. Why do you think there are so many branches and sub branches?*

Human life isn't long enough to study all branches.

Heaven: Yes, in order to study all branches, one has to take all the lessons, read all the books, pass all the exams, do an internship, make practice and then become a speciulist. As time wasn't enough for all of these, a task division had to be made, the horizontal expansion method called as branching was adapted. In this way each branch focused on its subject.

DENTIST

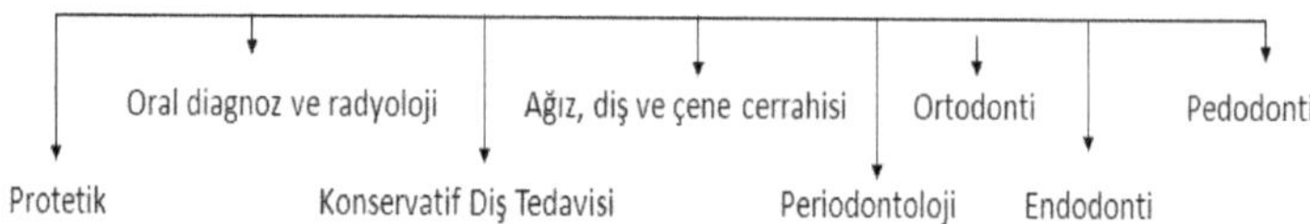

Prosthetic –Oral diagnosis and radiology-Conservative Dental Treatment-Oral, Dental and maxillofacial Surgery, Periodontics, Orthodontics, Endodontics, Paedodontics.

Branching that requires specializing in one segment, was a horizontal solution for the blockage in perception based science. Additionally, mankind needs someone who has knowledge about each peace and who is able to connect them.

How will be the vertical version?

Heaven: *You will see soon. In order to find the reason of the blockage, phases of knowledge are taken under observation according to the "How does it Function" question.*

With the increasing knowledge and experience level of the united people, relaying knowledge and experience to next generations, reinterpreting and improving knowledge and experience has become a relaying race. There are two basic criteria affecting the success of this race:

1.Human Life

Imagine the education that should be taken and the books that should be read by the scientist who would improve knowledge and experience of united people in an environment where communication instruments like internet and television rapidly in-

crease, hundreds of books and articles concerning each sub branch of each discipline are issued. When childhood, old ages and the time spent in sleep was abstracted, it has seen that remaining time was not long enough to educate a good scientist. Methods like speed reading techniques, early education for children, weekend classrooms, summer schools, private lessons, making sacrifice from childhood or spare times which could cause serious damages in human soul have been tried besides branching.

2.Rate of Transfering Knowledge and Experience To Human Brain

(Learning/ Teaching) In order to learn experiences and knowledge before him , a person should perceive and transfer knowledge to the brain by reading, listening, smelling, touching or watching, process them in the brain and share the data and the results with others.

Imagine yourself reading a 200 page book in 20 hours. Your eyes transform book pages into visual electrical signals and relay them to visual cortex nerves during 20 hours. Visual signals transferred to the visual cortex of the brain with speed of light are recorded in the memory as processed digital data after they are identified with your knowledge in the past.

You can enter the same book into the computer approximately in 20 hours by using a keyboard. Once the book is transferred to the computer, it's transformed into a digitally encoded electrical knowledge. It could be opened and be looked at over and over again, modified or copied to another computer within seconds upon request. The book that has become digital could be transferred to other computers within seconds via flash disc or e-mail. For the human brain which works like a computer, reading a 200 page book in 20 hours and transforming it into digital knowledge that could be perceived, is logically same with entering and recording the book into a computer in 20 hours with a keyboard. While both of them perceive a non-digital 200 page book from outside at a slower rate, once the book is perceived the processing rate actualizes in speed of light. When a person wants to recall a part from the book, he recalls the recorded part of the digital book in his memory within seconds just like a computer.

As it's seen in the examples, brain is a biological computer using digital (electrical) data. In order to learn things we have to transform knowledge into digital form. As knowledge and experience that should be relayed to the brain increase, speed rate of perception of five senses remained same. Speed rate of getting knowledge fell far behind the speed rate of the increase in knowledge.

The strength of a chain equals to the strength of its weakest link. Speed rate of our perception system equals to the speed rate of our five senses.

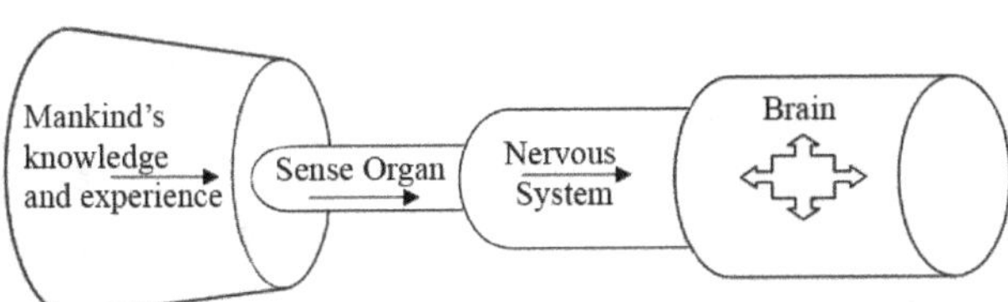

It is often said "we only use 5% of our brain." If our nervous system and our brain work fast, and our sense organs function at a slower rate, how can our brains function at full capacity? This means that we can only send inside 5% of the information received. Since this situation has continued for a long time and the area that sorts out meaning has slowed down in an effort to adapt, that means that our situation is bleak, indeed.

Once you enter a 200 page book into a computer, you don't have to enter the same book into other computers. You can copy the digitalized 200 page book to a disc, cd or a flash disc or you can send it with e-mail. Wouldn't it be nice if transfer of digital knowledge among human brain working like computers was possible? I wish that a 200 page book which was read and digitalized in 20 hours could be copied to another person's brain within seconds.

The blockage in the perception based Science continued until the invention of the first electronic eye. Scientist who found out that vision had occurred in the brain, not in the eye, accomplished to copy the raw vision signal sent by the eye to the brain before it's interpreted. After that the electric signal loaded with the 200 page book that was sent to the visual cortex by the electronic eye was copied to a computer.

In this way, a digital copy of the 200 page book has become transferable to another person's visual cortex within seconds before it's interpreted. Scientists have accomplished the transfer. With this invention, transferring knowledge from one person's memory has become easy just like transferring files from one computer to another.

Instead of transferring raw knowledge, wouldn't it be better to transfer the memory record of someone who raise awareness with the best interpretation?

Heaven: Raw knowledge doesn't involve sensual and emotional images. When you learn things told by the authorities concerning knowledge, patterns might form in your memory which could be hard to overcome. You might find your brand new ideas worthless if they haven't seen by the scientists before. Therefore, your right to be you, in other words your right to make contribution to knowledge with your self-consciousness that hasn't been formatted yet, will be taken away from you. Previous time periods and interpretations are given after a certain phase.

When electro chemical movements of the neurons, communication sense and codes in the brain- the biological computer- which makes calculations by using electric, thinks and decides, were solved, communication in speed of light has been accom-

*plished among human brain without sense organs. Thanks to direct communication, speed rate of learning which has increased to the speed of light, has been the first step triggering the expected vertical breakthrough. From then the most important objective of science was to solve the electrical codes of emotions and thoughts that occur as measurable and electrical activities as well as making brain's patterns. Brain transforms things into brain's language. Because of this, a **World Brain Dictionary** has been prepared in order to establish communication between world and brain.*

Thoughts, words and pictures were interpreted. With the decoding of the digital code of the memory where memories are recorded, human memory became readable, duplicable and modifiable. **World Brain Dictionary** has been prepared. As everything has changed so rapidly suiting to the vertical breakthrough, mankind was caught quite unprepared to the first phases of Holographic Reality which has started with the transformation of emotions, thoughts and memory into digital signals loaded with knowledge.

Computers aren't interested in knowledge source just like the human brain. They open according to the memory records in their hard discs. If we take out the hard disc of a computer and put it in another one, the computer will open according to its new memory and reflect the content of the hard disc on screen. As sensorium of the brain isn't interested in signal source like computers, when it awakens with another person's memory, it will behave like him. Of course,

these developments bother people. In this case, those who solve and capture the system can play with people's pasts, that will ruin soul balance and corrupt beliefs.

*Heaven: That's why it's called Divine Knowledge Age. As I said before, new answers lead to new and deeper questions. You said **"Those who solve the system will manage it. It is not important to solve the system but to endure after you solve it."** If it was an unwanted phase in Divine Design, God would never give us this opportunity. As HE gets closer to us by opening the door, HE lets mankind to pass a different level to make us understand him, we thought. Hence we were given this opportunity, we spent our energy on thinking how to use this opportunity for the benefit of all.*

Every scientific invention has mundane and holistic purposes. For example, as electronic eye makes visually handicapped to see in mundane dimension, in holistic basis, it enabled to establish common memory with the solving of human brain. Don't you think that God wants us to speed up after this phase?

You are right. We see the clues of these things in films, books and documentaries for years but we usually call them sci-ence- fiction and don't take them seriously. As our priority is to deal with the problems of the present dimension, we don't give importance to these superior knowledge which seems to be useless for our lives. What do you think about those who don't watch tv?

Heaven: *You made a good point. Mankind thinks that Divine Knowledge or superior knowledge will come from spiritual or divine sources by those who have miracles. New knowledge and awareness is required in order to reach advanced knowledge of higher dimension without solving basic secrets of the world dimension. Everything you can think of including people, films, books, newspapers, animals are knowledge sources. We are preparing mankind for the big transition for a while by giving transition knowledge via books, films and documentaries regularly and progressively.*

This is an open invitation for anyone who takes this seriously. We tell them about the whole adventure under the light of science. Taking television away is not a solution. You should watch new knowledge sources including films, documentaries, scientific discussion programs instead of watching soap operas, news full of violence and fear, marriage programs, football commentaries, magazines and useless competition programs. Don't forget, those who get away from communication, get away from knowledge.

All the scientists that you watch in the documentaries present you all the knowledge to you in a concentrated form, which they have collected over 20-30 years through the researches, lessons, conferences, seminars. Is there any simpler method to transfer knowledge? The science and the technology of the system is hard and requires advanced knowledge while its principles are so easy. A person who watches documentaries for a few months can learn the basic principles and technologies of the universe.

We send our knowledge for the whole humanity. Everyone receives the knowledge in its raw form and give it a meaning by interpreting it through his knowledge and intuition. The invitation is sent for those who understand it.

Therefore you must have developed a system for the inter-brain communication as well.

Heaven: as you know, there is basic communication in computers; it's the Windos7 system which makes sense of the clicks of the mouse or the letters you press on the keyboard. And you also download the programs and information they you would like to use. The basic operating system for the humans (breathing, the movement of the heart, digestion) such as Word, Excel, PowerPoint etc. or AutoCAD, SQL-Server etc. is the information he brings by his birth through the genetical codes. Go out and communicate with people, nourish your soul through different sources. Be in contact. Do not allow yourself to be dry up because of feeding from one single source...

How was the Collective Memory established and charged with? Does the electronic eye first read the books and change them into digital codes?

Heaven: It is not necessary for the electronic eye to read the new books. the books prepared as word documents, are directly sent to visual centers after being turned into digital books. after the individual memories were solved, we established the Collective Memory network and direct it for the good of all through the

*COUNCIL that represents the **Unity of Ideas.***

How do you ensure absolutization?

Heaven: for something to be absolute, it should give the same results in every circumstance. Just like 2+2=4 everywhere in the universe. (also called universal). It hinders the possibility for humans to have absolute decisions when they change them for the sake of their friends or relatives. Since the computers do not have human sprits, the individuals consist only of database. It doesn't matter if you or another person does it when it comes to computer work.

the centers of perception in human brain are not interested in the source of the signals. They just do their work. They are like humans but they don't have family or group connections as they are not humans and they aren't interested in humane matters.

It is a teacher whose decisions are absolute and who works constantly to teach and train. Everything is under the control of the computer, not even a single leave moves out of its scope. The illusionary scenes in Dreammatic and Thinkmatic are like dreams seen jointly with the computer.

Neither was it born from something else nor gave birth to any-thing else. It was just made of the existing material and thoughts. Its provisions are absolute, its decisions do not have any emotional connections and always give the same results which rest on objectivity. That's why all the power and man-agement were turned into monopoly and the machines were ac-cepted as the fairest of all the judges.

REMOTE CONTROLLED HUMAN

I don't know how it was for the good of the whole but things promised to us thousands of years ago and can be considered a fantasy of science fiction are turning into an increasingly convincing reality. As I said before, the distinction between the real and the illusion has become indistinguishable. All my ties to my reality of the world are about to be severed and there is no turning back from there.

If the sensoria are not responding to the source of a signal, implant receiver/transmitter chips in the sensoria. As wire-less signals, transmit the perceptive signals such as images, sounds, smells, tastes, touch and such that you want one to feel and make the human live in the reality that you like. Hard to swallow but a human can become remote controlled in an instant.

In this case, those inspecting a remote controlled car's engine, hood or the roads that it took will take a while to realize that it is remote controlled, as they won't take notice of the wireless communication system installed in the electronic assembly which we call the brain of a car. At that rate, the soul can not reside in the human body.

Heaven: Soul commands the body like a remote controlled car. It is not the car itself that remotely controls it either. Just as in computer games, it only maintains an online communication with the car. As the car knows what to do with the signals it receives, it is sufficient to transmit signals to the car remotely and to receive the feedback on what the car did afterwards and determine new commands, to be the soul of the car.

That the soul transmits sending/receiving signals to the body that feels utterly real won't put the soul in the body. It is merely the proof that the connection is vivid and convincing.

Anyone who decrypts the signal code of the car can then transmit to it and drive it anywhere or stop it. The receiver circuit in a car knows how to handle the incoming signal but isn't concerned with the source of it, it only does as it is commanded. Just like the human brain! Then how much human is a remote controlled human? Who or what is -or are- the remote controllers?

Heaven: How much human is the one that has yet to grasp what one is and is supposed to do but merely follows advice such as "conquer your ego, love everyone, show forbearance" and, without thinking things through, ends up loving the wrong ones, showing forbearance to useless people and lives with heavy emotional burdens? Won't these emotional traumas prevent one to live one's self?

"I make a fool of myself, all because of you, all the time!"

You are right but should we not love everyone? You both tell to love and criticize for loving the wrong people without thinking it through?

Heaven: When told to love everyone, it's not meant to let everyone into your personal life, into your bed! It's meant to refrain from taking sudden emotional decisions to become destructive due to being carried away in prejudices from past records in your subconscious, to show forbearance. In other words, "Do not decide how and with whom to live before you understand what you are living in". As Rumi said of people and events, "Only through the mills of the mind should you let things on the vessel of the heart".

HOLY GRAIL: HUMAN BRAIN

What you said reminds me of a good proverb I read years ago in a study book for the driving exam: "Do not punish a passenger in the wrong with death". I'd rather be a wise lunatic than a blissful ignorant. As I understand, human brain is the Holy Grail in this case!

Heaven: See there! As your knowledge and perceptions increased, so did your awareness along with your feelings and thoughts. **Congratulations!** *Yes, human brain is the* **Holy Grail.** *The essence of all teachings, advising "The answer is within", "You have the answer", "Know thyself" was the assertion "Search for the answer in your body, the answer is hidden in your body". Sadly, as everyone had long been seeking the answer only in the soul, scorning the body as representing ego and overpraising the soul, it took thousands of years to see the remote control mechanism implanted in the body.*

It is quite normal for a system that takes its power from being undeciphered to cover Divine knowledge with something worldly in order to preserve its mystery and power.

Heaven: As the God has used the best method there is for con-

cealing the answer, that is hiding in plain sight, humans have kept seeking the answer through conventional viewpoints, in subatomic particles or in the depths of the space and in the end, got stuck in the universe between the microscope and the telescope. Likewise, we sometimes give the key to set them about seeking the door and sometimes the door, to seek the key. Back when you were a child, you wanted to be an astronaut, do you still want to?

And how! It's my biggest dream to go to the space. I've wanted a space rocket in the garden of my workplace for this.

Heaven: *Then it will do good to go outside for a stroll in space for a while.*

I can't recall how long it's been since I came here but can I call my mother first? I call her every day but I haven't since I've arrived here, she must have been worried.

Heaven: *A single day here corresponds to a 1.000 years in world's reality. Therefore, it's only been a few seconds since you've arrived.*

How do you mean?

Heaven: *No how of it; how many days is 1.000 years: 1.000 x 365 = 365.000. Then, 1/365.000 is a little bit higher than the light/electricity speed of 1/300.000 which we call the brain's processing speed. Everything here happens at the speed of light and since the illusory scenes we create in your brain occur at the speed of light, is it not normal that it's only been seconds? If* *you like, let us calculate how many minutes, how many seconds have passed since your birth. You are 48 years old. In that case, that makes 48 x 365 = 17.520 days. You are in Thinkmatic.*

Since 1 day is 365.000 days by Divine calculation, 17.520 / 365.000 = 0.048 days. And since 1 day is 24 hours, 24 x 60 = 1.440 minutes and 0,048 of 1.440 minutes is 1.440 x 0,0048 = 6.9 minutes. If 48 years is 6,9 minutes in the world dimension, then it is only a few seconds here.

While the matter disintegrates at the speed of light, thought, meaning information, will not. When we connected the human brain directly to the Dreammatic and Thinkmatic, all working at the speed of light, dreams and thoughts of the humans, surpassing the speed of light with their illusory bodies, were freed. Come now, it's time to travel in the space!

Now this space travel will be a truly extraordinary experience. Suddenly, we found ourselves inside a space rocket waiting for the ignition. After the countdown, our rocket took off with a terrific noise and following serious turbulence, it went up past the atmosphere; hurray, we were in space now. I was so eager to quickly unfasten my seat belt and experience the sensation of emptiness. Finally, we got into orbit and I unfastened my seat belt, took off my astronaut suit and started about watching the world, the sun, the moon, the stars and the distant galaxies through wide windows with an indescribable feeling. Meanwhile, I was floating around in astonishment, as if flying like Superman. In space, everybody was the Superman.

I don't know how long it took me to get used to this mind-blowing environment and get back to the training after shaking off its impact but, without getting carried further away by what is visible, I decided to line up my theories and questions about the space. I have a few to ask, shall I ask them now?

Heaven: I should quickly take those initial questions in your mind now so that we can reach the questions and answers born from the free mind of a person experiencing this environment for the first time. Please be comfortable. You can make serious contributions to the **Collective Conscious** *by asking a question never before asked or also through a comment never before made.*

First, I love this point of view of yours. *"Please be comfortable. You can make serious contributions to the Collective Conscious by a question or a comment never before asked or made."* **The way for a human to feel as a part of the whole; that will be by feeling that one's words, thoughts and action are regarded as a whole and that one can contribute to the whole. A few years back, the result of a study I researched after taking an interest in a very intelligent kid who played games on the computer and the phone all the time was thus:**

"Kids who are constantly subjected to one-way information transfers such as "Don't do that but this! Don't go there! Do it like this!" at home, at school and everywhere and whose opinions aren't asked, have been found to struggle in self expression. Therefore, they love and form an attachment to computer games that take them seriously where they could choose the troops, the tanks and the weapons they like, and fire and move them when and where they like, be the authority, in short. " **as was told**.

Quickly, I started finding games or planning pursuits that she too could join, put forth ideas and express herself where we would spend time together. The time she allocated for computer games decreased. Very special talents and character traits started to surface one after the other. Just like in here, life started to become more colorful, fun and educative for both of us. Love is sharing and the most precious thing to share is time, to spend time together.

A whole where I don't contribute and I am not regarded is not my whole.

Heaven: Collective means "that which forms by the gathering of all persons, living and objects of all levels". Collective Conscious is the sum of the Individual Consciousnesses and the most important aspect of it isn't being a simple recording device that brings together all the consciousness but an artificial intelligence of super intellect that can evaluate all the recordings and constantly expand through learning by itself.

When we say "we were inspired by the God and designed it for humans", we don't just mean it in a technological sense but also in a spiritual one. It was not a God that only watched but one of action that also evaluated, punished and rewarded that was in question. One likes the idea that the God would value and take all aspects of humanity seriously and track them all on an individual level. Think of it this way, each of your prayers is a petition in the unity of God to change something about yourself. Perhaps you don't notice but if you are praying, it means you believe in being a part of the Divine unity, that your petitions are valued and that there is the possibility of your wishes coming true. Isn't that to unite yourself with the unity that you feel you are a part of?

Maybe you will like it at first but won't it become boring? Won't it be discomforting to have an observer watching, evaluating, punishing and rewarding you all the time?

Heaven: *Why should you be afraid if the evaluators will not be bribed or commit injustice?*

SPACE: GOD'S ARCHIVE
PARALLEL UNIVERSES OR DREAMS?

If everything is an illusion and death is waking from sleep, why do we have fear of death?

Heaven: *As a necessity of creation, you adopt that which has obscure origins more readily, and love that which has an unknown end more thoroughly. We only look at what that fear of suddenly losing what you have, called the fear of the death, can propel you to do and sometimes use it to motivate you. A heart attack or a minor injury is sometimes used to distract you, sometimes to make you appreciate your life or that of others around you and sometimes to call attention to what you are living in. Now, let's take your questions about space:*

- If merely a sun and a few planets are enough to sustain life on earth, why the extravagancy with all these stars, planets

and the like?

- If mankind will enter heaven merely through good morality, why is the seemingly (+) infinite macro-universe or the seemingly (-) infinite micro/nano-universe of the space shown to us?

- By showing us a space consisting of such superhuman scales and distances that are humanly impossible to use, is it meant to tell us "you should only focus on your world and don't even think about ever making it out of there or solving the universe"?

- Seeing as humanity feels helpless like a drop in the ocean upon this visage, don't you agree that it is a case of disproportionate use of information?

Heaven: As with every subject, there is a problem of asking the right question regarding space as well. When faced with something seemingly superhuman and physically immeasurable, humans usually regard the unknown and the unsolved as a question and intensify their focus on it. While some come up with superhuman answers, others produce seemingly logical solutions that are otherwise based on consensus.

Yet some others accept that "the unknown can only be solved with the heart, namely divine love, unconditional surrender and when the time comes, one will be shown what one needs to know" and they wait in patience. Those who recognize the Divine strength in the depths of their souls and live through unconditional surrender will say "I will not be given a burden I can not carry nor a question I can not solve" and ask the right questions to find the secret hints and arrive at the answer.

The answer will appear when the right and the sensible question is asked?"

Heaven: Prone to cling to a power beyond themselves, humans are inclined to leave both the thinking and the decisions to others. Therefore, they have lived on through history mostly as captive souls for they haven't paid attention to whom or what they have surrendered in every period.

Because they have succumbed into prompt and unconditional submission without utilizing logic and without seeking the right questions that control their reality, humans have worshipped an assortment of gods such as god of fire, of moon, of sun, of cows; and have arranged their lives around them.

Logic is not a control system that hinders love but a beneficial one that prevents it from getting out of control and ruin lives. Do you think it is sufficient to just believe and to go with the flow (as if on auto-pilot) and then to wait for your development to progress? You need to make an effort at understanding in order to believe, and to practice forbearance in order to surrender.

I am very patient. If I believe, I'll wait.

Heaven: If you understand patience in the context of fatalism as not doing anything, just letting everything slide without making any effort and waiting, then you have to put up with such hardship which you may have overcome with very little endeavor. At this stage this is not patience, but putting up with. Do you think that told you to just sit and wait around? This is a story of real love, sharing, exertive and exemplary to fatalism.

One day they said to one of the sabaoth: "What is the difference between those who just talk about and love and those who live it?" The sabaoth replied, "Let me show you." Firstly, he summoned and set a table for those who couldn't plant love to their hearts from their speech. They all set to their places. Later, hot soup arrived in the plates together with so called sabaoth spoons of one meter long. The sabaoth had a condition, "You should be eating by holding the spoons from their tips." They all agreed and tried to drink. But what happens? As the spoons are too long they cannot drink without slopping around. At the end they realize that they are failing, they get down hungry from the table.

Thereupon the sabaoth said, "Now, let me call those to dinner who know love truly." Those who came and sit around the table were people full of light with bright faces and eyes shining with love. This time, when he said "go ahead", every one of them held the spoon from the tip and plunge it in the soup and reached to his brother across the table, thus helping him to drink. In doing so, each one fed the other and they finished the meal being grateful. Thus said the sabaoth, "Whoever sees only oneself in the table of truth and plans to be fed, he will be left hungry. And those who think of one's brother will be fed by the brother undoubtedly and don't you ever forget, those who always win are the ones who give and not take." Another result to be drawn from here is that; "Those in the table of truth will say that they have no freewill, and say this is fate, not using his wit to find solutions to difficulties and Show any effort will stay hungry physically and spiritually. And those who use their wit for finding solutions and show effort will be fed physically and spiritually.

As you understand, patience is not stopping, not losing hope, but waiting hoping, trusting, believing and showing effort. Do your best, use all your sources, work hard, show effort. Undoubtedly, those who win are the ones showing effort and not the ones waiting. As Niyazi Misri says, "This is your page, fill your own life."

Because I understand patience, as the Satyagraha method referred to in the book of Non – Violent Resistance written by Gandhi. *"One must declare the truth one believes and by not showing any violence to anyone must be ready to die for it."* **Or "Everywhere is like a desert to me without you, because I am thirsty for you and I cannot drink water from any fountain" kind of, "I am not interested in another choice!", I thought.**

Heaven: Our aim is to give an opportunity to those people to Show who they are and what they really can do by constant thinking of what to do for a better World, find solutions, show efforts, keep their faith and believe. And as Gandhi is a successful practitioner taking his part in history setting an example to the generations after him will inspire as a guru (mentor).

I remembered a nice anecdote regarding making efforts:

An old carpenter was at his period of retirement. He mentioned to his employer, the plan of his retirement from his job and liv-

ing a more free life with his wife and enlarging family. He will obviously miss the payment he received every month. However, he was in need of retirement. The contractor was sorry that one of his good employee was leaving, and asked as a last favor of building him another house.

The carpenter accepted and started the work, thus it was easy to see that his heart was not at his job. He made sloppy craftsmanship and used bad quality material. How unfortunate was it for him to say goodbye to his devoted career!

When the work was done, the employer came to review the house. He gave the key to the house to the carpenter, "this house is yours" he said. "It is my gift to you." The carpenter was in shock. How he was embarrassed! He wished to know that the house he built was his own. Would he do it that way!

It is the same for us. Each day we build our lives. Most of the time, we do not give our very best to the work we do. Afterwards, we understand that we will live in the house that we built and go into shock and say, "if I can do it again, I would do it very differently." However, we cannot go back.

You are the carpenter, every day you pound nails, place a wood or build a wall. "Life is a do it yourself (DIY) design," said someone. With the behavior and choices of today, you'll build the which you will live in tomorrow. So, build it wise. Don't forget: "Work as you do not need any Money, love as you have never been hurt, and dance as nobody is watching you."

When I said, how does it work? It Works integrated with billions of brains in real time, handling all their recordings at the speed of light, questioning, and updating like a computer and a software of a superhuman system is needed.

Heaven: As I just said, we may ask the same simple questions for solving the systematique of a system that doesn't make sense to you for space.

1.WHAT IS IT USED FOR? You should say, what is space used for. When you look from a humane perspective, it doesn't seem to be useful for humans. Well, if it is not useful to the humans then may be it is useful to its Creator. Why does the Creator made space and why does He shows it to us?

2.HOW DOES IT WORK? If we cannot answer the question of what is it used for about anything, then to be able to understand we instantly pass to the question of "How does it work?"

If you'd like, first we shall see and enjoy the beauties of the space, and after a break we shall begin our lesson. For example, what do you say if we look through your reflections and life recordings in space? Shall we go around space a bit?

To my space records?

Heaven: It cannot be explained. You must see, and live it! (as soon as she said that our spaceship was near the Sun. We were looking at our boundless World with no boundary lines seen from near the Sun.

At a screen in our spaceship, the block of my house, Street and we started focusing to my home. We were looking at me sleeping in bed. "First look at the watch here, then the watch there." I looked to both of them. In the spaceship the time was 04:38, and in my room it was 04:30. As you see, an image in the World arrives to the sun in 8 minutes. So, someone looking to earth and to your image sees your condition of 8 minutes earlier. (Then suddenly we came to the Chan Chin planet and the World was no longer visible. The watch at my wrist was still at date / time ... /03/2014 04:38, on the screen it was 30/08/1988, 16:00 hours and we were at my graduation ceremony.

We are at the where the image filled light is which set out from earth on 30th August, 1988. I can easily see every moment while moving the ship back and forth by changing the distance to earth. After the graduation my mother, father and aunt Aysel, all our graduation celebration and so on, I can see whatever there is. It is similar to a DVD player where you may push the rewind and forward button to watch the part you like over and over again.

Shall we go to my childhood?

Heaven: *The ship is at your command and you only need to think the moment to which you want to go.* (Without thinking, I wanted to go to the Sunday meals and family gathering in my grandmother's garden which was filled with flowers, fruit trees and full of chicken in the pen. I was playing with the sword of my grandfather Hamdi, and was stroking our horse of Thrace in copper Brown with a White diamond mark on his forehead. I had everything to make a child happy.)

Well, shall I look at the recordings of someone I have never seen? For example, I do not have any memory of my grandfather Nuri who died long before I was born. I will be pleased if you'd help me.

Heaven: Normally, no one can look to another's private recordings besides the attendants, but I shall make an exception for you. (We came to a very far away place from Earth and so, it wasn't even seen as a dot from the earth. It appeared in the screen a scene from the childhood of my late father and his father, my grandfather Nuri. I was watching my father's childhood, my grandmother and my father's communication with them like a documentary. Going back and forth, I could watch the parts I chose on my grandfather's image recordings. There were time lines about everyone in space like film strips).

Are we now traveling above Levhi-Mahfuz?

Heaven: We are above Levh-i Mahfuz if you think of it from a two dimensional perspective. But if you think from a 3-D perspective, we are traveling within the Cosmic Memory (the digital space) and only above your records. We aren't making a time travel. We are just traveling above the past records.

Do not restrict time travel only to getting on a vehicle and going with a speed faster than the light. Now let us think about a day you were in your grandmother's garden. The plum trees have just blossomed and you are on the tree, did you remember?

Yes I did. What a nice childhood I had, surrounded with wise people.

Heaven: So, as you think of something you lived in the past, images are created in your mind, you actually reach your records here and load this raw vocal and the visual records into your memory. You are not here but you basically bring this setting into your memory as information. There is not much difference. The result is the same whether it's you going there or it, coming to you.

Are the secrets of Atlantis, Sumerians, Mayans, the Egypt pyramids, Prophet Moses, Jesus, Muhammad, Şems Tebrizi, Rumi, Atatürk and Fatih Sultan Mehmet who contributed the Collective Mind also recorded here? How much can you go back in time?

Heaven: The light reveals what is concealed by the darkness and brings its knowledge to us. The light, besides illuminating, also has the faculty of transferring images and keeping the information in its quarks. They use light in space because of its ability to transfer the information. The light in space means visually loaded information. We reached records that are approximately 13.7 billion years old. The records of those who made a contribution get published in history books and legends as a gift of encouragement.

I found the best example for this subject during a visit to a memorial museum in Jerusalem (Yad Vashem) that was enacted to commemorate children who died in WWII. Thousands of small mirrors (about 10 x 5 cm.) are suspended on transparent strings in a dimly lit room. Because the strings are of the same color as the room in the low lighting, the mirrors resemble a path passing through the middle of a barely visible room.

In one corner of the room are five candles in a circle placed at certain angles to the dim light; the mirrors reflect thousands of candles which give the feeling that the dead children are stars in the sky. As you walk through the room, the reflections from the candles at varying distances cause you to feel you are in space. You don't see the mirrors unless you look carefully and you think the candles are real. You assume that they are different candles when you see the same candle image from different angles. Bu t there are actually five candles in the room. Why are there so many stars? What are they used for?

Heaven: The energy source should be in the same form as recorded by the recorded. For example the energy of electricity is required to protect the information in the hard-disc since the energy of electricity is used in the computers. If the electricity level of the hard-disc is not re-charged at certain intervals by turning on the computer, the information in the hard-disc begin to get lost in the long-term. The space is an hard-disc that works with light. The light in space is a light loaded with information and its energy is required to be renewed at certain intervals. The stars are the sources of light which provide the required energy of the light. Each star ensures that the information is maintained by not changing the level of light in its region.

If our location in space is a reflection of the date and hour on earth, then we are actually changing our places on the fixed time line in space and the time is fixed in space. Actually all times are experienced simultaneously in space considering the logic of multiple users.

Heaven: While you are living one moment of the 24 hours in a day according to your location, the other moments are lived simultaneously in other places on earth. A person looking at earth from the space seems like he is seeing and living the 24 hours simultaneously.

Since all of our worlds past is recorded on the space-time line, a person looking on from outside of space, can watch the complete past as it is recorded there.

To a person looking on from space, the centuries are all experienced at once. *Someone who is moving away from the world will be (+) or (-) direction in worldly time compared to its speed on the time line that records in the speed of light.*

A short example will be of value here. Let's think of a car and a kilometers-long train both going in the same direction.

If the car travels faster than the train, a person in the car will begin to see the carriages that are toward the front of the train and if it goes slower, he will see the carriages at the end of the train. If the car and train move at the same speed, the person in the car will see the same train carriages and it will appear as if the train is not moving. When the car stops the person will see all the train carriages move past him.

At a fixed point in space, (i.e. Venus) a person looking at earth sees the frames of a film of the earth speeding by like the carriages of a passing train. Space is taking photos of the earth at the speed of light, just like a camera. The time is fixed in each frame just as in a normal camera.

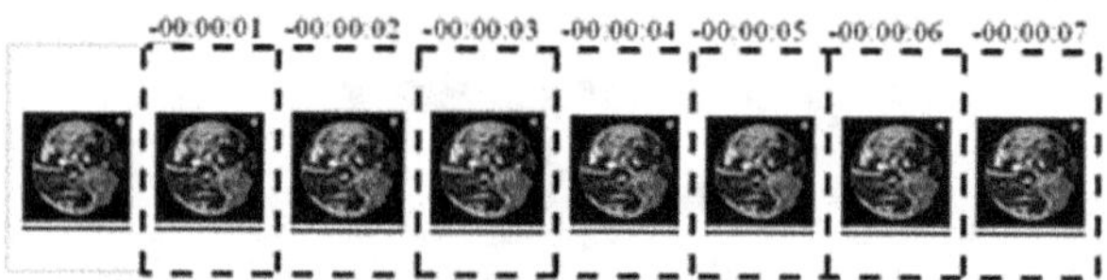

A person traveling in space, seems to be traveling on a path made of the film of earth's past. A person looking at earth as he moves away from the earth at the speed of light, is like the person inside the car which is going at the same speed as the train. Therefore, to a person looking at the world while moving from the earth at the speed of light, the image of the world will become fixed and (because the time change is zero) time will stop.

So someone who travels in space can change his location over the records of the past as he is traveling. So since the space is a 3-D recording device, where is its read/write head?

Heaven: You are the computer programmer, where do you thing it is? Do not forget that the space is a 3-D recording device! A movie is recorded on a two-dimensional DVD. The piece where the head is found, reflects on the tv screen visually.

 Since space is a 3-D recording device and there is life only where the earth is, the read/write head has to be on earth. Just like in DVDs, it will be live (active) where there is the head and not live (passive) where there is not. How about the authorization?

Heaven: You think the world moves in space with the energy it receives from the big-bang. Yet the world is moving as a read/ write head just like the fast trains that slide on air on a magnetic line.

Millions of people can make searches, contributions or arrangements simultaneously, just like it is in the internet.

What do you do if someone bypasses the firewall?

Heaven: A bright and penetrating light will immediately go after him to catch. The space is shown to you as a clue of what you are living in, not for you to feel yourself weak and lonely in its vastness. Each time you look into the space, you look into a 3-D system which has recorded 13.7 billion years and still continues to record. The light is knowledge in space. It is the light state of the knowledge.

So the space is the Cupboard of Archive of its Creator, it is the Cosmic Memory, the hard-disc of the Collective Mind. Was it also recorded when I had experiences in Dreammatic?

Heaven: Hologram is holistic recording. Everything is being recorded fully. Your experiences, your thoughts, and even your dreams...

Is there another life in space? Are there parallel universes?

Heaven: This is one of the most difficult technical subjects. Was Dreammatic a physical setting?

No. It was an illusionary place you created in my brain. It was kind of a dream.

Heaven: Good. When we say that it has multiple users, we talk about a system that works through being connected to the same source by means of different and independent contents.

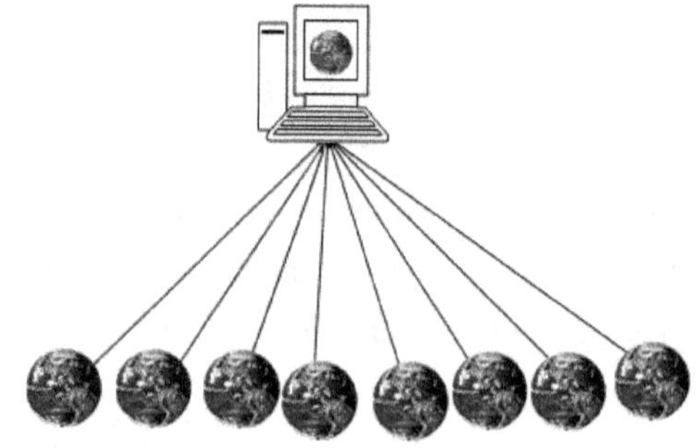

Predictions based solely on space cannot go beyond classical predictions. "In such a vast space, there must be other universes. They are so far away that we cannot see them, or they are very close to us but we cannot see them because they are in a different dimension." Once it was understood that space is the system's recording device or hard drive, our focus shifted from space itself to the technology and management of the system that operates space.

Thousands of people get connected to Dreammatic simultaneously and each goes after what they see in their brains as created by Dreammatic. That's why we call the Parallel Universes as 'Parallel Dreams'. There is a personal illusion of universe in each person's brain and he can only see the dream universe in his frequency. Feeling others and reaching their universes require serious authorization and awareness.

The transient world, the transient universe and the transient dream all made sense. The life is a dream and aren't we each living in a dream of a different illusionary life?

The transient world, the transient universe and the transient dream all made sense. The life is a dream and aren't we each living in a dream of a different illusionary life?

While I'm in space, I want to share a dream that came to mind on Earth. If I were to design a place of worship, such as a mosque, church, synagogue, etc., I would create a dome that evokes a sense of space, walls that convey a feeling of in-

finity with deep space imagery, a floor that is partly carpet and partly glass, and beneath the glass, again, deep space imagery. In short, I would plan a mosque that feels like praying in space, with a space dome, walls that give a sense of infinity, a glass floor, and appropriate lighting. Thus, instead of praying in an earthly place of worship, people would feel as if they were praying among the stars, as if in the presence of God.**

The mosque could be named "Sky Mosque" or "Mosque in the Sky." This mosque, which everyone, local and foreign, would want to see, could be planned as a museum outside of worship hours, with the revenue generated being used for a social project.**

Cennet: Let's put it in the public section of Shared Memory, maybe someone will apply it by granting copyright. **Just being part of such a project is exciting for me.** (Meanwhile I realized that we were approaching to earth coming from the depths of the space. The borders of the countries became more visible, I was viewing the political world which had become scattered through the borders drawn by the politicians.)

THE SUPER-HUMAN MADE BY THE HUMAN

Why is the world divided in borders?

Heaven: This is not the world, it is Thinkmatic. It is a mental lab to measure how this gift affects you and to decide if it is you who uses your gift or your gift using you, rather than to observe which gift you have. (I interrupt to ask)

How are the records made onto the Collective Memory evaluated?

In the Collective Memory, not only are records made but also all recorded information gets processed and evaluated by the Central Intellect right away. What their dreams are, the set of illusory stages created for them, the actors, the content, they are all directed by the Central Intellect.

Exactly right here the condition of super-humanity steps in. For any human being it is impossible to inspect and evaluate all this data at the speed of light. Even with an evaluation committee, the necessary speed would not be reached and due to humane reasons, a unanimous vote would not be reached in decisions. This has to be done by a super-human being rather than a human. What happens in the Dreammatic, what you say about the Thinkmatic is truly super-human. How do you administer this system, are you a super-human too?

Heaven: Can you define super-human?

The one capable of humanly impossible things. Creator of everything in the universe. Also the one doing humanly things with a speed, greatness, smallness and correctness that are impossible for humans. The one who sees, hears, records and evaluates what happens in the whole universe and who can do it for each person, separately.

Heaven: *Let us change the question; can the human do something super-human? Can mankind make super-human systems that are superior to humans and work in speeds and sizes impossible for humans?*

Like God? God forbid!

*Heaven: The saying "Frogs at the bottom of the well would think stars in the sky are as big as they look from the well top" is a good description for those who try to interpret today and the future through their limited knowledge. Please do not attribute everything super-human to God without thinking the issue of super-humanity through. The **Big Awakening** will come true when mankind- always made look at what he cannot do instead of what he did and will do- will see he can and does know more and abandon self-denial.*

Focusing on what you can do, say "What don't we know?" instead of "What do we know?". Don't be a frog at the well's bottom. Think like a super-human to understand the super-human! Think from a broader angle, honoring human dignity. Once you

158

find the divine knowledge inside you and feel your own strength, you will understand and perform the super-human. Just like the ones before you.

What do you mean by the super-human accomplishments of the ones before me? How can I imagine what I don't have? It must be something different from everything I know, or else I would have known it before I looked for it.

Heaven: Didn't the mankind who supposedly cannot do anything super-human create yoghurt, jam, pickle, bread, heaters, coolers, cars, buildings, planes, habitats , space journeys, space stations, in short a second alternate nature that we call the Parallel Nature by interfering with nature and reproducing what it gives? Parallel Nature is the effort of the mankind, the owner of the earth and sky, to redesign the earth and to reshape the vessel instead of taking the shape of it. You should see what people shaking off their Neutral Element syndrome has achieved and can achieve by focusing on what they could do and not what they couldn't. Super-human perceptions are not needed in order to understand the super-human. If you can pass beyond the shell and reach your own essential knowledge while looking at developments in science and technology, you can see how close the technology is that created Dreammatic and Thinkmatic.

If you remember, I just said to look at everything by letting go of your ego. You called the super-human "the one doing humanly things with a speed, greatness, smallness and correctness that are impossible for humans". Imagine a lab doing hundreds, thousands of blood tests. The mood and exhaustion level of the expert evaluating the tests, the possibility of him making an error while writing down what he sees and dozens of potential mistakes affect the reliability of the results. Machines can make the same tests without getting tired and emotional, faster and healthier than humans.

Are you aware? We have left every decision to computers, from medical tests to identity researches, from accounting records to wage calculations to bank accounts. We accept computer decisions to be as valid as human decisions. In the current situation computers and devices have been transformed into human substitutes as reliable and independent devices in numerous fields. The decisions of machines that are extensions of human intelligence purified from emotions and that take samples, evaluate, draw and save conclusions **are as valid as that of a human at least.** *What do you think will happen when things go this fast?*

Computers and robots would be out of control and take governance, and then human vs. machine wars would start.

Heaven: *You are mentioning typical fears of the era of agent robots that educate, evaluate, punish and reward people rather than servant robots doing only what they have been told. Surely there is the possibility of such wars in a period when the intellect of machines will surpass human intellect and decisions of a machine programmed for human benefits will conflict with hu-*

man decisions. However, isn't it the human intellect betraying the closest ones and taking the whole world into war once it gets hold of power? This humane condition always takes place in every human creation. Isn't the humankind the biggest enemy of humans, too? In fact it is humanity's most fundamental fear about everything; the employee you trained and hired to do as you say getting out of control and acting as he likes, or your kid becoming an uncontrollable, ungrateful child not listening to your words and even giving up on you. Such fears exist in every area.

It is interesting that you make an emotionless machine like the computer evaluate an emotional being like humans!

Heaven: Do not think so greatly of humans. The distrust towards human justice has made it necessary to trust machine justice. Think about machines as never-exhausted, just human beings freed from sentiments.

How close are they to humans? Also, we couldn't fully answer the question "Why is Collective Memory such an important must?", can you answer it now if it is time? I am a software developer! I can easily understand and accept these issues. Please, be comfortable...

Heaven: *Human beings have succeeded in expanding their sensual boundaries outside the body by developing machines called jointed senses such as microscopes, telescopes, binoculars, measuring devices and infrared cameras. The first era was quite peaceful when humans had 100% control and machines lacking the laziness and tiredness genes used to work as **General Problem Solver** expert devices, doing only what they were programmed for. Mankind's attempt to exceed the boundaries of his normal creation, machines' ability to process loads of data and the revolutionary increase in processing speed brought machines to the next phase.*

A machine-entity with a frightening intelligence, capable of all human actions, self-aware, conscious and even emotional...

The real problem emerged when self-teaching and decision-making machines realized their own evolution, reached a superior intelligence than unsupported human intelligence and started developing better designs than humans. Thinking like a human, crediting human experiences and values, understanding human nature, being like a human but superior. The situation where unsupported human intelligence fails to administer machines of its own creation.

They acquire from you a new you, a "Machine-you". Has a machine-God or a virtual God been invented that makes people live in the illusory realities he created?

The virtual God is defined by the names Illusion God or Holographic God. Let's think about internet. Internet is a memory-sharing platform constituted by people who transfer the knowledge and experience inside their brain to a digital environment outside their brain and bring them together. The internet was very limited since the knowledge and experience input of human memory had to be done manually. Therefore only a very small portion of the knowledge and experience present in people's memories could be transferred to the collective memory of the internet. Consider the chances of reaching and possibilities of finding any subject you search for without using the internet. Collective memories transform human memory into a jointed memory by putting knowledge and experiences of others into service. Through this mental network we call ExitNet, one's memory becomes the memory of everyone and everyone's memory becomes one's own.

This far, Thinkmatic and Dreammatic are the names of the software or idea parts of ExitNet. What do you call the hardware, the material part of the system, and how is it administered?

VIRTUAL GOD AND MENTAL APOCALYPSE

Heaven: *The machine providing access to humans' most funda-mental secrets with its Thinkmatic and Dreammatic modules was called "Digital Mentor" or "Virtual God" at first. The complete machine that could create virtual counterparts of time, space, animate and inanimate beings via its super-human soft-ware and hardware has been called "**Virtual God**".*

Surely it is more important to command a power rather than producing it. So, mankind has formed the Collective Memory platform, i.e. jointed memory, multiple brain, multiple intelli-gence, multiple memory through assembling together the brains, intelligence and memories of all humans over ExitNet to provide the needed extra memory, extra intelligence and extra percep-tion. The Super Brain, the Super Intelligence mankind needs to command super-human systems with super-intelligence and su-per-memory. The "Memory Fellowship" where all searching and learning happens through thoughts.

Heaven: *Very good, you are no longer stunned. Now you can look further and ask "What can I do?" as the next step. You said "humanlike" in your descriptions. The machine is humanlike, but not completely human. The original always beats the copy. Machines cannot dream like humans do; pictures, music and art exist to imagine the dreams unimaginable by machines. The most crucial feature of machines is their disciplined work. Praying, yoga, meditation and sports exist to discipline the soul and the body that command the machines. It is a resistance training against all material and moral beauties or suffering caused by machines, seducing the ego. It commands the system clarifying the system.*

Following the harmless-looking question "What am I living in?" and answers changing all reality, I have to ask this though I don't know how convincing your reply will be. Do you control the illusion-signals entering my brain, whom am I talking to, to whom and which invisible structure am I surrendering, to you or to intelligent machines?

Heaven: *We might define this anxiety of the last era, a.k.a* ***"Mental Apocalypse"***, *of the world dimension as "not knowing what is approached while distancing from something else" or as the more common version "being scared of jumping out of the frying pan into the fire". While you drift apart from the current* *world dimension reality and approach the upper dimensional reality, you experience the restlessness of not knowing exactly what is being approached or passed beyond. Yet you cannot "climb the upper floor without stepping away from the lower stairs" as mentioned in the Divine Order and Universe book. Your position is discussed in Steven Strogatz' article in the book "The Next 50 Years" as "We can become the audience who is astonished by and cannot keep up with the machines they invented." We must join the machines, if we cannot defeat them.*

By inventing a machine and materializing his own knowledge and experience outside his body, mankind transfers himself into a machine. While teaching the machine to learn and make decisions like a human, mankind too will have to start thinking like a machine. Won't humans become machinelike while machines become humanlike in this case?

Heaven: What kind of human being will you become after the evolutionary process of the world? What kind of man does God want?

The kind loving everyone and everything created, not doing injustice to anyone, free from personal desires, following the rules and not committing crime, working for a better world…

Heaven: If you are aware of it, he wants loyal, hard-working, trustworthy and enduring employees, just like an employer. As if he will trust us with the earthly issues and give us tasks. You describe the perfect man as a robot without emotions and emotional fluctuations. As you said, while machines will become humanlike, human beings will also have to become machinelike and adapt their souls and bodies in order to command the superhuman power. If you cannot see the future, you are not thinking ahead. Now drop your taught fears about machine-human wars, wait for the process to complete and do not make misinformed interpretations before seeing the end result.

When human brain is "hacked" this way, everyone figuring out the communication of the human brain can connect people to this system and make them live in any illusion he wants. I can do anything I want in Dreammatic, but there is always someone watching.

When records are being used in public spaces with no privacy and with legal purposes for the greater good, there is no problem. Yet the power and authority to access all your information is still scary. Why not watch criminals only?

Heaven: Good morning, now you are waking up. Our aim is not only catching potential criminals, but discovering new gifts, knowledge and experiences and share it with the whole.

In order to be happy in Dreammatic and not pretend in Thinkmatic, one shouldn't know he is being watched.

Heaven: You are so right. Do you see now why you don't know where you came from and why? The success of the system depends on its secrecy and that is why secrecy is a must. Someone who notices he is being watched might drift apart from naturalness and pretend to influence the audience's decision. He might turn his life into a show and start to live according to the audience's preference. Thus the results would be inaccurate since we cannot measure their sincere thoughts.

A teacher in middle school had said "A true gentleman would cover his mouth even if he is yawning in a deserted pitch-black room." One who covers his mouth even with no audience. You cannot know if the man yawning and covering his mouth in a lit room with other people does it to look like a gentleman and avoid embarrassment or if he does it because of his natural behavior without going through the dark room test.

Yes, secrecy is the most vital condition in this case. The credibility of the system's decisions derives from the integrity of its secrecy.

***Heaven:** You can also think of it this way: Day represents presence and night represents absence. It is important to be the same person in both presence and absence. How would your father test the talent and diligence beside the trustworthiness and honesty of the newly-hired apprentice whom he will train and to whom he will trust with his shop?*

Trustworthiness, honesty and loyalty had always been more important than talent and diligence. At some corner of the shop he would leave a bunch of scattered, dusty bills, not once counted, looking like they have been forgotten a long time ago for the apprentice to see. On the days the apprentice wouldn't say "Master, I found some money here" he would check if the money was touched after the apprentice leaves. The apprentice would see the money in no time, the uncertainty would untangle either positively or negatively and the apprentice would receive his first degree trustiness verdict.

Various tests in other degrees would follow until the necessary trust has been formed. Naturally a wicked apprentice could know that the money was left as a test for him and pretend to be honest and say "I found money" disguising himself in order to reach his actual goal. You can never be cer-

tain whether or not someone is pretending if he knows that he is being watched. A total secrecy is crucial to be sure.

You can catch vicious people with a hidden camera, not a regular one.

People seeing the camera won't commit crimes and will pretend. However this is not only valid for money issues, but also for social relations. People who know they are being watched put on an act and behave as desired which makes it difficult to reach an objective decision about them.

Heaven: You are right. The camera indicates the observer, namely the audience. The observer effect is apparent in social media. People imitate celebrities to gain easy recognition.

They not only copy the outfits of celebrities, but also the ideas. Instead of writing their own ideas, they share already articulated and discussed words of someone widely respected, avoiding potential criticism. They choose this safe path to receive the attention but not the reaction of their followers. Doing what is expected in order to preserve the follower's live attention and waiting for social approval triggers pretense in people and they cease to be themselves.

How do you provide such secrecy? How do you interfere with human perception? Aren't some people aware of being monitored?

Heaven: Through a sort of hypnosis called tactile illusion the way people interpret perceptions gets temporarily reprogrammed. You are in a state where you have no autonomous power; you cannot pretend or imitate and can only act through your true essence. You are made to believe that there is no observer and consequently no fear of prejudices and being judged. You let your most beautiful dreams form in front of you through the illusory scenes capturing your imagination and shaping everything you would dream or think of.

Those who through super-detections based on intuition noticed this illusion and shared it in their works have made history. They failed to name it as holographic or virtual reality, but aware of the illusion, they defined it as "Finite World = Finite Reality", "Fantasy World", "Dream World" etc. What is belief, if it is not exactly this? Intuitive detections where there is no logical or concrete proof. The fact you know something although you don't.

Frankly I have been irritated by the idea that my brain can be programmed with simple switch-on and off buttons. I am

struggling. Why did you need such a system, what compelled you?

Heaven: You said in the Dreammatic "Such high technology couldn't have been produced for mere property, sexual fantasies and gluttony". Can you think of any other reason?

It is possible to program the Dreammatic with seemingly never-ending material and spiritual suffering and turn it into Fearmatic. If it happens, it functions as a very good educational system that motivates through punishments and rewards, evaluates the hard-working and non-working. You reap what you sow.

Heaven: It seems correct from the perspective of plain logic. Then let's begin with a more basic question. Do we agree that the world is a school and we are here for our evolution, spiritual maturation in other words?

Of course. The level of material and spiritual knowledge and experience gradually increases and evolves. Like in every educational system there must be those who pass and those who fail.

Heaven: Imagine that you are a teacher at a school now. You have two groups of students: one working to receive the prize and one not to repeat the class. Which group do you think would become useful people in the future?

Surely the education that rewards the ones working for the prize, i.e. success.

Heaven: *Punishment, namely motivation through fear. If all depends on the results, anxiety will drop success and quality; the concern for result will damage the process. After a while fear would take control and you would end up doing as you're told by the anxiety booster. Pretty prize, big fear, high obedience.*

Reward-conditioned goal or profit! In this case the way to success, namely the goal, goes through finding the control chart affecting the teacher's decision and acting accordingly as a well-behaved, hard-working pupil. Completing the numbers, passing the class and collecting the reward would be enough to show one's strong belief. A character not working unless there is a profit or turning to those who can provide the highest profit.

Prize and punishment trigger the feeling of security. Not going to hell and not losing the heaven force a person to a constant internal calculation. Once carried away by the control over the course, you will chase numbers of merits and sins, making your life a living hell with the fear of the past. "Doing good and receiving good in return" is an act based on benefits. Fear or re-

wards make you do something you don't like, whereas you do what you love voluntarily.

*Praying is a method you can use to find your essence. If you turn faith and prayer into numbers and chase them while applying the control chart of the creator, you cannot find out the essence of faith and prayer, therefore you can neither grasp your own essence nor comprehend God. During your effort to follow the control chart, God wants you to find yourself and be yourself through working with your reason, instead of being motivated through rewards and fear. Heaven and Hell exist in order to understand which one of them motivates you. Our favorites are the people who **possess their own motivation**, who work for the whole, for the entire humanity. As I mentioned earlier, not only the result, but also the way you could or couldn't come in first or how much strived will count*

You know, sometimes during a race some athletes stop to help their fallen rival up and miss first place. They do miss first rank, yet they conquer the hearts. Rewards such as chivalry and sportsmanship await these special people and special occasions everlastingly. As you can see, there are no winners or losers in Thinkmatic, the perfect preparer. Through this system we call expectation management, we try to determine the boundaries of their personalities and talents, the breaking points rather than whether they are going to win or not. We don't wish to burden you with tasks and responsibilities you cannot bear and upset both you and ourselves as a result of wrong expectations of you.

Why need me, if my breaking point is lower than others?

Heaven: You know what is done with children who dislike, fail at and don't want to go school. They will be taken from the school and placed as some master's apprentice. But is his chance of self-realization and becoming successful lost? Of course not. He only gave up the safest and more success-guaranteed road. It is always possible for him to work hard with a good master throughout the years and turn into a very good master, an invisible hero of society. Like the ones who discover the defect of a car by merely listening to it while it works, repair it straight away and raise good masters like him. Like Master Yahya who evokes admiration through his positive, wise and inspiring conversations with you while your car gets repaired... Or for instance Master İbrahim who both paints the walls of your house admirably and adds some soul with his color preparations. What matters is that you put some of your soul in what you do, not which way you take or which job you do. That you are a wanted and loved master, engineer, doctor, lawyer, laborer, boss.

Imagine people's living conditions in all around the world. On one side there is the modern era including advanced technology and wealth, on the other side people leading a primitive life in Africa's savage tribes... Keeping societies in other continents in mind, you can discover a lifestyle of almost every period among advanced technologies and the most primitive society.

Almost like each period is experienced at the same time.

Heaven: Because the knowledge and the experience in Collective Memory is re-experienced, researched and improved with new results at every level. Newborn grow up experiencing all stages of history. Based on the talents and the level of endurance of everyone, fields and stages they will work within the whole are determined. It makes people unhappy to work in easy or hard jobs, below or above their talents and capacity respectively. In short, everything is set up to know you. You just passed a little exam of attention and you had no recognition of it for corrections.

What do you mean, am I in a trial during learning?

Heaven: A way of keeping the attention alive during education is to provide wrong or incomplete information to the students to measure how well they are following the class. I am repeating the part you missed: ***"Our favorites are the people who work for the whole, for the entire humanity."***

What is the problem here? You are saying that the wholeness of humanity, that it is favorable to work for the entire humanity. A most lofty goal.

Heaven: You forgot a very important thing. The wholeness doesn't consist only of humans but also of all living outside humans, like the animals, plants, trees. Here we see the social/clustered shape of ego. Yourself or those outside the cluster are worthless. When you care only about humans for the humanity, you are not trying to understand and are missing what the nature is trying to tell you. If you look through your worldly ego; animals are the servants of humanity beneficial to us for their meat, milk, wool, transport, communication and the like. If you escape your worldly ego and look again; (1) Nature takes only as much as it needs. A lion won't kill all gazelles. A tree won't drain all the minerals in the soil. If you are not sharing what you have in hand with others, it means you are taking more than your fair share. The most beautiful sharing is the one done at the source where you don't take more than what is your right. (2) You will see another inspiring engineering aspect of God in all of it. Now, let us ask the most fundamental question:

WHY DID GOD CREATE ANIMALS,
WHY DO ANIMALS EXIST?

If God were to create animals to sustain the basic needs of the mankind, God would have created only the animals whose meat, milk, egg and strength we benefit from. And instead of having a pair of all animals taken into Noah's Ark, only those animals we benefit from would make it in.

Experts say that the lack of communication is the primary cause of violence. And the primary cause of violence against animals is to see them as mere animals, to fail to properly perceive the reason of their creation and their place in our lives.

You might be surprised to find that animals were not created only to be loved and to be fed and how they inspire health, science and technology, how they ease your life and in short, what you have learned from them and what more you can learn.

To reintroduce the animal kingdom to the humans, let us ask the question "What state would the mankind be in without the animals?" Maybe those in the animal kingdom, entrusted to the mankind, are not merely animals, what you do think?

From now on, I will strive towards a unity inclusive of humans, animals, plants; all the living in short. **And we, humans, are superanimal for them!** *Henceforth, I will pick food leftovers for the animals in shelters and bones from butcheries for the strays.*

Heaven: It is just as vital to try and find food for animal shelters, bones and leftovers for strays, in other words participating in active field work, and to join activists pressing to pass laws and bills on animal rights but these can not be the only ways to protect animals. "You can not drive a windmill with a pair of bellows." As long as the locals fail to see the stray cats, dogs and the birds as living beings they ought to share their neighborhood with and to protect, state of animals will be up to personal efforts. When the cats, the dogs and the birds in the streets become the locals' cats, dogs and birds, the problem will have been resolved. For those who love animals but don't have them as pets at home, it's a beautiful resolution to love and feed the ones out in the streets.

I think of it as a deficiency of knowledge arising from not knowing their contributions to our lives to see animals as just random animals.

You should come up with ideas to bring about a new beginning to human-animal relations. If animals necessitate bills and physical precautions for their preservation in a country, then the educational system must be put under review urgently. There will be something lacking in one's soul who has not experienced love for animals. While on it, let me share a cheery example on how cats and dogs view their owners:

Dog: *"Considering it keeps giving me food, provides for my needs and protects me, it must be my God"*

Cat: *"Considering it keeps giving me food, provides for my needs and protects me, I am most definitely its God"*

My trial with humans have been supplemented by a trial with animals, trees and plants but it turned out well. There could not have been a unity without them. How are the exams specified in Thinkmatic?

Heaven: In your opinion; is it harder to preserve honesty and integrity among the good and the righteous people as in the convent of Rumi or in a place without justice where swindlers live in wealth?

In a place without a modicum of justice, of course.

Heaven: The school of development called Thinkmatic is an illusion consisting of the hardest trials testing the talents and the breaking points of a human. Did you think that you would reach your own truth without passing through the trying scenarios of Thinkmatic that many have passed before you? Joy to those to preserve in their faith and to persevere to the benefit of the whole without straying from righteousness.

First the Thinkmatic, and then, as a reward for those who work and forbear, the Dreammatic!

*Heaven: No, **Dreammatic** the first, **Thinkmatic** the next, and then **Dreammatic** again, so the cycle goes.*

Alright, why are there boundaries?

Heaven: How the traits we have detected in you through the Dreammatic have affected or will affect you, we can only evaluate in a context with others present as well. For instance, Heaven and Hell are choices offered to find whether you are motivated by fear or reward. The best I can try you is with your opposite. The way to see the justice in you is to drop you among the unjust. Thus, the level and the severity of what is inside you and its effect on your life and your choices can be measured.

While in Dreammatic everything around you is shaped up as you imagine them to be, everything in Thinkmatic is shaped up by us to the benefit of the whole and is put at your disposal. There are rules if there are boundaries and there are also trials if there are rules, right? Think of the physical boundaries in the world; each nation has laws and rules to follow. Additionally, there are moral boundaries like faith, consisting of invisible borders, laws and trials independent of physical borders.

Therefore, the world sized boundaries, laws and trials we call the Thinkmatic will be filled with different scopes and contents at every stage for your culture codes to be deciphered and the development scenarios determined. We shape Thinkmatic together in accordance with needs and talents and then put this simulation of earth and sky at your disposal to see which one of you will do a better job.

How do you draw out the hatred in a person? You keep them alive in a dream (of a war started by your predecessors, turned into a blood feud where no one can win) between the extremist groups of race, religion, nation, city etc. With respect to scenar-

io, social hatred is boosted by bestowing the supporters of war with awards, praises, heroic status etc. The subject is constantly measured to find whether he or she will give in to the hatred of the group while gradually becoming an emotional supporter or, he or she will listen to the voice of his or her essence and become one of those trying to maintain and establish peace.

However, these scenes of injustice are not for us but for you to be just. Never give up on your own justice in these scenes where you are expected to get carried away by a heightening of your desires. Because it is your justice being tried, not ours and what we measure is whether you can respond with justice to an injustice laid upon yourself. You will know that even a withered flower will bloom if you speak to it with love.

There, you are the flower in the pot. Always love yourself so that your light shines brightest, always send your love to an injustice so that it heals. By using the power of love against injustice and working for peace and charity, you must strive towards a better world.

THINKMATIC BEGINNING CRITERIA

Is the reason for people chasing money and power in the world a struggle to get everything they want and to have anything they want made in order to turn it into a Dreammatic where their wishes come true?

Heaven: Precisely. Endeavor of a person, grown used to the fulfillment of any wish in Dreammatic, to transform Thinkmatic into the Dreammatic might, sometimes, turn into an uncontrollable ambition. The most important reason of this is the lack of love.. Think of it this way; someone about to go to the airport has baggage that is difficult to carry and too little money. She could take a taxi, airport shuttle or bus and metro via 3 or 4 transfers. As she doesn't have enough money for the former two and after showing up at the airport in sweat and tears following arduous transfers between public bus and metro with luggage in hand, she might think to herself "I will work hard and be someone who earns enough to take a taxi the next time" and decide to become richer when faced with her financial failure in order to expand her area of effect. From now on, her primary goal is to earn the power to take a taxi, namely the money. To afford a car, to command, to hire cleaning, all done to feel the power and as she controls it the more, the more she feels safe. In the end, money is the only thing you own.

On the other hand, if she has a few friends to call and ask "could you drop me off at the airport" who then will do so, she already is rich. If the ambition for assets and position is not to benefit humanity but to govern and acquire, it is merely the struggle of the lack of love., of lonely people who believe nobody will be there in their hour of need and are afraid to love. The reason for desiring power is to maintain a staff of friends when in need of attention and help. Yet, they put up with it not out of friendship but out of the need to look after their own loved ones as per their job. Exchanges based not on love and respect but financial obligation.

A lot of people have the belief that the more the material means, the more the happiness. The supposition that those with 1 degree of happiness on a salary of 1.500 TL will have 15 degrees of happiness on a salary of 15.000 TL. Yet the problem lies not with being powerful or rich but with how you use and share that power. What makes a place a heaven is those inside. It is the where and the who you are with which that matters. If you are living and working with people you love and who loved you, you feel safe and peaceful. For you personally, for them, for ALL OF YOU in short, everywhere is truly heavenly. It's not heaven but Dreammatic where everything is in your control and everyone serves you.

You might recall that Dreammatic is exclusive to the person. It was asked if there wouldn't be a ruckus to determine whose wish to be fulfilled in the presence of more than one. You were silent and acknowledged. Isn't it the same for the world? Imagine people with different desires living under the same roof, could they be happy? Imagine them with common goals and getting happy over the same things, isn't that house a heaven? Wouldn't the world turn into a heaven, now tell me where the heaven is?

In my opinion, what matters is not where but with whom a person is. That is, where a person is with loved ones is Heaven. Some get close to God and feel Heaven by inventing something, some by writing a book, some in a house with a

spouse, a child, a dog and a bird. In this case, who determines what manner of state and with whom I will enter Thinkmatic? How are the beginning criteria designated justly?

*Heaven: You have arrived at the subject everybody struggles to make head or tail of, which we call the **Beginning Criteria** or **Beginning Energies**. How is it determined who will be born in which country, which city and which neighborhood and to which family and when, or in short, where and with whom? How is Justice In Beginning and Divine Justice maintained in the Beginning Criteria? Why am I poor and he rich? Did I want to be poor, to be handicapped, to be born in this family? etc. Similar questions largely unanswered for the majority and classic answers such as 'why would I want to be born in this country, in this city, in this family? Who would want this?' Yet, it's not where you begin your life which that matters but what you build upon it and where you take it to.*

To those who ask "Did I choose this life" in this world. ☺ I always used to say "How do you know you did not?" Laying the responsibility on somebody else is the easiest way to escape responsibility. I have all my blockades wide open, curiously waiting to hear your answer for how the Beginning Criteria are determined!

Heaven: Let's think of Adam and Eve; the man and the woman who have arrived at the world simultaneously from the divine plane. What state were they in upon their arrival?

They were separated and pleading for God's forgiveness.

Heaven: Well then, why were they separated and why were they pleading?

They had eaten the forbidden fruit in Heaven and as a punishment, they were banished from Heaven and were landed separately on the world. They kept on pleading for reunion and to return to Heaven.

Heaven: Had they not eaten from the tree of the forbidden fruit despite God's direct admonishment, would they be landed on the world and separated? No. So that when they disobeyed the only restriction in Heaven and committed a crime, they ended up designating the beginning criteria in the world. Just like our designation of the beginning criteria of Dreammatic and Thinkmatic. It creates illusionary environments where people feel 100% lonely and safe, shaped by the needs of their souls. We go even further than the jugular to observe and to record their experiences, committed to their hearts' contents, in order to build personality simulations and thus, designate the beginning criteria.

Example; we send someone of the opposite gender to measure what the subject will do to what lengths and how much he or she will bond; we only initiate it and leave the control to the subject. We prepare scenes to draw out to the extremes the things called bodily ego from within the depths of her soul that not even she herself knew of. We enter the character traits detected in Dreammatic as the beginning parameters into Thinkmatic.

an active spiritual measurement through methods such as mind-reading, implantation of feelings and thoughts and healing-oriented scenarios, we apply psychological incentives. That way, we get to measure the limits in all kinds of environments on an individualistic and holistic scope.

Dreammatic is like the prep class to Thinkmatic.

Heaven: Actually, they are both prep classes to each other. Similar to the designation of the professional branch you will study based on your scores while studying in the prep class of a business high school to measure your aptitude towards prospective professions. What weakness you have in your character, what your strong points are, your talents on all the fields we know, your sub talents, your abilities and breaking points are all measured. Do you settle with what is offered where you believe everything is to your liking? Do you have the ability to adapt to change and manage and improve opportunities? To even say "let's have that too" is an ability to manage in Dreammatic.

I'm having a difficulty grasping what goes on in Dreammatic, why does everything turn out the way we want or why are we given that sensation? How does the beginning and progress happen?

Heaven: Beginning Criteria and the free will is the stage hardest to understand and to accept, therefore we will talk on every detail until they are grasped. The environment where everything is to your liking is where you have the control, feel safe and take hold of the world around you in any way you like. A person's beginning state in Dreammatic is like a baby's first years in the world. Just like in Dreammatic, the mother, the father and the family try to understand the slightest gestures of a baby to appease and to provide for his or her needs. Such that;

During the postpartum period, if the mother manages to connect with her baby with affection and understand the baby's needs by the gestures and the sounds, they will establish a bond of trust. And the **baby, relying on** *the mother, will find the opportunity to explore his or her surroundings and developer her or her abilities. As the development of perceptive and motor skills and the mental, emotional and linguistic development of a baby is very rapid during this period, it is very important to ensure that the baby is faced with a wide scope of educational experiences with visual, auditory and tactile stimulation such as people, toys, items, animals, colors etc. Only this way will the neural networks in a baby's brain develop rapidly and the mental development will be positively affected.*

We establish a sincere relationship with the person in Dreammatic and evoke a feeling of confidence such that he or she can share anything. As such, we enable them to explore the world and provide opportunities for them to react individually so that they can experience true behaviors and different roles to their hearts' contents. How would you get a sense of someone's tooth who has never tasted Turkish cuisine?

I would take her to an open buffet restaurant with Turkish dishes and see what she picks and what she likes.

Heaven: *In case you didn't notice, you left no room for change, i.e. contribution. Imagine you put all the cooks at her service and you have her try out a few dishes every day, giving her the prerogative to make all kinds of changes, like telling the cooks how much salt to use or what to serve with which dessert. By allocating 100% of the kitchen resources to her management, you will derive at previously unknown tastes to develop for you both.*

*Through new combinations and new methods of cooking, you will have added new tastes and flavors to dishes otherwise consumed as is. We call this system of developing while overseeing development, where both sides learn new things through new experiences while teaching something to someone, **Know-Know** or **Learn-Learn**. How would you define yourself?*

Pilgrim of truth, decoder...

Heaven: What if I were to ask, can you meet the prerequisites of the journey?..

Willingly.

Heaven: Most people you would ask this would commonly say yes. But to be a pilgrim of truth requires true will, forbearance and endurance. Few have been able to see to the end of this training.

Did those who succeeded become the chosen?

Heaven: Not chosen but the entitled, those who excelled in their own categories. Everyone focuses on the Beginning Criteria but there are also the Result Criteria. The state of the personality simulation on its way out of the Thinkmatic. Numerical values of all favorable and unfavorable traits are shown on graphics.

Seeing as I am here, am I a winner?

Heaven: You are on a training that's yet in progress.

I thought I was contributing to the Collective Memory by everything I have ever done on the world dimension. Therefore, weren't certain stages supposed to be given to me?

Heaven: You contribute to this system both from within and from without. Everything you resolve on the world dimension is resolved here as well. I can illustrate it like this: you can run a survey on how to better design an airplane by flying distinct passengers of all types of profession, faith, different pasts and the like and collecting their impressions. All the passengers on the plane will support the redesign internally. There are no redundant passengers on a plane and everybody's opinion onboard is necessary to make better planes. The most unexpected person might bring the most unexpected perspective for a better design and he might not even notice that himself during his life.

And there is a staff of engineers onboard the plane who shares the passengers' experience vis-a-vis who will apply the information gained from the passengers' experiences to new designs of the plane. A technical staff, whom we call the system inheritors, to carry out the maintenance and work the new designs for the continuity of the airplane factory. And the system has to raise its own personnel from within these systems. The technical staff applicants passing through the Thinkmatic and Dreammatic examinations, initially unaware of being watched in their veiled memory, will commence their training here with conscious journeys after passing through those stages. Those who will inherit the book will be interested in subjects on solving the system and their search for knowledge and learning about the future will never end. The first trial for those to get a seat in the management of Thinkmatic is to find their way out of Think-matic. One who can't make it out of the labyrinth cannot design a labyrinth.

Do I have some means to watch my trial that enables me to be here? Please, I am utterly curious. Plus, it will motivate me that much more to see them succeed.

Heaven: *A nice reminder for you to understand the system as well as a short recess.* (In a flash, we ascended up into space. This time, we went far further than my previous space recordings from a moment ago. We were at least a few centuries back. I was very surprised to see me in a period from centuries ago.)

You said "we were inspired by God, did for humanity" **for this marvelous technology Was it from the sacred books? Could you elaborate a bit?**

Heaven: *Not just the sacred books, we divided all the ancient knowledge, wisdom and intuition brought down to all the peoples into groups. Sociological Verses or Sociological Information for all the subjects regarding daily life on earth and worldly matters, also including sins and merits. And we called it the Technological Verses or the Technological Information for the verses explaining the technical subjects such as the creation and design of the universe. Later on, when we brought our findings together with technology, we saw the foundations of the Sacred Design.*

As I recall, the subject we treated in your training in 2009 was Technological Verses and the technological design of the universe. The Sacred Design I wrote in depth in my book "İnanmak İçin Yeni Sebepler" ("New Reasons to Believe). What is the subject of the training this time?

Heaven: This time, by learning the foundations of the Sacred, you will commence transcendence from World Dimension to the upper next dimension of reality. How would you describe the infinity of God?

Trillions of stars, an infinite universe, an infinite amount of superhuman diversity and order. The doors to the superhuman realm!

Heaven: That is what you will see if you see God with your worldly ego. However, God's love, as well as God's clemency, is infinite. What does an infinite clemency mean?

Infinite Forgiveness. Dispelling of sins through repentance!

Heaven: Isn't that a self-wise angle yet again? To repent is to apologize. It means "I have tormented my true essence, I regret my deed; I will not make the same mistake again. I beseech an opportunity to show my remorse, I beseech redemption". The finest example to it is The Prophet Moses. Moses accidentally murders a man and, regretful, pleads with God.

God has acknowledged the penitence of this servant of Him, who has committed a crime in the world and, without waiting for the Day of Judgment, has forgiven him while still in this world and has elevated him to the highest rank possible, making him a prophet.

Clemency and forgiveness is a choice with serious benefits when practiced at the right time. It could also lead to calamities when practiced before a person has matured and become regretful enough.

I seek refuge in your for forgiveness to ask; how will I make sure that you only want what is good for me? How will I trust you?

Heaven: About infinite clemency; infinite opportunity means infinite tries, infinite opportunities to show yourself. Think of the infinite means and choices presented to you for you to be able to discover yourself and to be able to succeed. Giving you the opportunity to succeed in any condition without any prerequisites, any preconditions, even without a necessity to trust God. Likely that God seriously puts trust in you, right? We provide the people in Dreammatic and Thinkmatic ample opportunities to succeed and to self-improve by passing them through trials on different levels of knowledge in different periods.

NOT REINCARNATION; DREAMCARNATION

So you have succeeded in reincarnation, then?

Heaven: Actually, it's not exactly a reincarnation. As you know, hypnosis is an imaginary reality that completely leaves everything outside to provide a heightened focus. Brain can be reprogrammed by tinkering with senses during the hypnosis or sleep. Make someone in hypnosis listen to a loud melody along with the smell of rotten fish while previously listening to a quiet melody along with a fragrant perfume. Thus, you will have reprogrammed the brain by assigning two smells to two melodies.

When you wake them up and have them listen to the respective melodies, you will hear them say "does it smell rotten fish here?" or "I get a touch of a fragrant perfume" even though there is no smell. As you can see, we can load a smell to a melody and leak into the brain and manipulate it. Reactions can easily be steered by manipulating the learned subconscious reactions.

So you have hacked the brain...

Heaven: Let's say we just stumbled into one of the doors left open for us in a section of neurological security. It depends on what you understand by hacking. One can easily reprogram another's reality from without as well. Example: Close your eyes and imagine taking a lemon off the fridge and slowly cutting it in half, squeezing the juice into a glass and now, slowly drinking it. Is your mouth wet yet? If you were affected, it means I played with your perception. If you cry, be scared or get excited during a picture in the theatre, it also means your perception has been played with.

Even a cup of coffee will affect the brain. We call this Hacking from without. It is done daily and easily to the uninformed through elaborately selected words, colors, sounds and other things with the help of media and the press.

During hypnosis, the same is done from within by hacking the brain. We reprogram the brain again and again by managing the dream center through imaginary realities found in the information and emotions of dreams that provide a heightened focus.

*As we maintain experiences on the artificial life forms over and over again in dreams, we call it **Dreamcarnation** instead of Reincarnation. The name of Reincarnation here is Dreamcarnation! Think of your dreams, what you make of it when you face what you had just seen in your dream the day before? That you visited the future?*

I feel as though I had the same dream twice. The system is hinting at me, I think to myself. In fact, I think that I am not alone, that I am given support through hints.

Heaven: This is what we call the conscious recurrence. To relive the future you have seen or predicted. Simulation determines your reality, what you have lived in Thinkmatic shapes your real life and you live through it. If you are ready, we can watch a Dreamcarnation that tries, not your memory but your intellect.

If my dream center becomes like a three dimensional computer screen controlled by a computer. The illusionary

scenes in my dream are constantly collapsed and restructured, just like a computer screen. This is the most I have ever been ready! I am ready, let it begin...

TRANSCENDING NIRVANA

Heaven: The name of this test is 'Transcending Nirvana'. You made a serious leap in this crucial test; it would be very useful to have you watch the recordings of your mental journey which included the tests of physical endurance, intelligence, courage and determination that you have completed successfully at the Thinkmatic.

Considering that I have lived centuries ago, was I a pilgrim of Truth feeling a burning love inside for the Truth?

Heaven: Truth seekers or pilgrims are not only dervishes. Dervishes are the conscious pilgrims of the truth. The Truth Dimension, where all the answers are revealed, embraces everyone and everything. Everyone lives and strives in a certain part of the truth. Everyone who works with passion including the scientist, the housewife, the shopkeeper, the policeman, the soldier or the farmer is a seeker of the truth, whether conscious or unconscious. Sometimes they are aware that they have found pieces of truth and sometimes they are not. A conscious truth seeker called the Guru, immediately sees the spark of truth in someone that he cannot see in himself.

The test, is a journey which was named as Nirvana thousands of years ago. It was told that it was in the east, somewhere no one

196

has been and come back to this day. It was a place whose distance was unknown, but described as "impossible to reach". In a time where there were no roads, we provided an opportunity to walk from Istanbul to Nirvana, and you accepted this invitation which sparked an excitement in the depths of your soul. With a group, you set off on the journey to Nirvana. Let's watch it:

We set off with a group from Istanbul to find a place whose existence is believed in, but known to be unreachable, Nirvana. As the correct direction was not known, we had to take the route travelled by others before. We travelled in very harsh conditions for days and months, staying at the inns of those who gave up travelling further and became innkeepers.

Physical fatigue, hunger and thirst weakened our faith and eventually our sense of purpose, which caused a dissolution in the group. Some friends were influenced by the suggestion of the innkeepers most of whom said "How can you reach a place that does not exist, there is no need to continue. It's better to lose the saddle than the horse. Look, we stopped here, we established good friendships, we are living together happily and in peace.

Come and join us, don't ruin your lives for nothing." So the people in the group began to return to Istanbul declaring "This is it for me. It is pointless to go any further.", or decided to set up a new life there by following the suggestion of the innkeeper.

After leaving behind the inn where the last of the friends have given up, I walked alone on a land with no signs. I walked so long in this boundless area that the idea of a Nirvana began to feel ambiguous. No one searched for what they could not find. If the target was unreachable, why would I suffer this ordeal? I doubted if I had given up my life in Istanbul including my friends, the successful career and the family as well as the happiness that could have been in my life, all for nothing. The question of God, and the answer of course, could not be easy. However I was motivating myself believing that he would not use a disproportionate force like asking college level geometry to primary school students.

At a point where all my aspirations perished because of the continuous threats and obstacles on the road, I reached an inn at the side of a deserted forest of dense but dry trees and shrubs, where no animals or even no bugs lived. It was a place which set one's teeth on the edge. The innkeepers hugged me and said that I was the first person to reach there in centuries, with a slight pity upon seeing my exhaustion. They were the descendants of a generation who arrived there centuries ago and became innkeepers believing they could go no further thus naming the place Nirvana.

They had named this peaceful inn **Nirvana***, which was located on the boundaries of the dead forest. Reaching Nirvana had made me extremely happy, and terribly sad. It was really nice to have found someone to talk to after those lonely months spent on the deserted places, and to be able to sleep in a safe place with a soft bed and clean sheets, having access to clean water and food. Nirvana was worthy of its name; it was a place where hopes and excitement have ended for the pilgrims. Very peaceful and happy people lived there. As usual with very peaceful places, there was neither a new answer found nor any excitement felt there. This was nothing more than an inn which offered tranquillity to weary souls. I believed this place should have been called "The Inn of Tranquillity". The caring manners of the beautiful, kind and skilled girl they had assigned to take care of me, quickly got me back on my feet. Those at the inn lived happily and peacefully with the rightful pride of having found the furthest inn on the road, even if not a new answer. For the first few days I experienced feeling the rightful pride of having reached this furthest inn. However, having experienced that harsh and adventurous traveling for months, peace was nothing but the last thing I was seeking for. The Nirvana Inn, inhabited by those people who had lost their excitement and let themselves into a 'peace-*

ful' sleep out of the despair they felt about passing the forest, soon became unsatisfying for me. I thought I would have never set off on this journey if it was only peace that I was looking for. There was a fatal forest challenging me ahead, and behind me was a path I had walked for months enduring all kinds of hardship and poverty. I was stuck in Nirvana between the two.

I understand that our ancestors were pilgrims as well, who decided to settle here as innkeepers after being defeated by this forest. So, is there another inn further ahead? Is your inn the last one on this way?

*"Ours is the last according to what our ancestors had told us. None of those who came here could continue in this deadly forest even when they tried in the daytime. As none has ever managed to reach it, we call it the **NOTHINGNESS** dimension where no man has ever set foot before."*

There were flashes in my mind at that moment. Those who had acknowledged it as an impassable forest and lost their hope were unintentionally ruining the hopes of newcomers. Maybe their greatest fear was to lose the chance to deserve the title of having travelled the furthest to someone who had the courage to go further. The more effort you show for something, the more attached you become to it. It turns into a hope for you, which makes it difficult to renounce. It is the hardest thing ever to bury hopes into despair. Having endured the painful journey with the hope of reaching Nirvana, I had no chance but to continue. Those Nirvanians who were living in peace as having born into this despair had no reason to seek what was beyond since they haven't take pains to endure the exceedingly painful ways to reach here. What they lacked was DEVOTION; the devotion to reach the Truth Dimension.

As Rumi stated, since the goose egg placed among the chicken eggs was never told that it could fly, it thought it was a chicken and never attempted to fly. For those who have been born in a cage, it was hazardous and unsafe outside. Their ancestors had killed all the excitement and hope in them. That reminded me of a test made in an aquarium. Imagine you split an aquarium in to two with a piece of glass. The fish in the right half of the aquarium hits the glass barrier again and again to pass to the left side. It is observed that after the glass is removed the fish still behaves as if the glass is there. This is called learned helplessness.

Those in Nirvana needed to overcome the Learned Helplessness they felt about passing the Deadly Forest. It was impossible for them to consider passing this forest before overcoming the feeling of helplessness and experiencing the awakening. The glass in their case was the forest. Perhaps the elders, who might have tried to keep their children away from the forest had claimed: "This is the furthest point that can be reached. Those who have achieved reaching here do not need to do anything else. We just wait for the time to come. When the time comes, we will be amongst the limited number of successful ones who will be taken by those that will come from the other side of the forest."

To tell the truth; at a point when my determined spirit was looking for an honourable excuse to give up, having no energy to take another step after all the distance I had travelled and the hunger, thirst, fatigue and fear I had experienced, my tired soul had adopted this option for a while, which offered an honourable withdrawal.

They said: "Beyond is the NOTHINGNESS dimension, here is the final stage. No mortal has ever gone further than this. It is impossible to go beyond. There is no way to proceed. We have to wait here for those who will come from the NOTHINGNESS dimension to take us."

In this place where everyone kept waiting, no one could suggest that there may be another inn ahead, or question why they did not try to reach beyond. It almost seemed forbidden to propose such a suggestion. It is only asking the right question that can free one from the obstacles that block his path. So I started to dwell on what the question might be that will remove the mental blockage between me and the truth.

Resting and eating healthy food relieved my exhaustion and despair which encouraged me and flourished my hopes. When the extraordinary circumstances returned to be normal, my mind began to work properly again. It's been long since I had turned down the possible chances of peace and happiness offered by a standard way of life, for the sake of this path. Sometimes the path you left behind obliges you to travel ahead; turning back was now much harder than going ahead for me... My happiness was beyond this forest and I had no choice but to go through it.

Whenever I glanced at this forest of death, I felt a wild excitement, a wild yearning that drew me in. The moment I realized that I disagreed with this comment "the forest is impassable", I knew it was time to set off.

Courage and hope enabled me to ask the right questions that will lead me forward. And I asked, how far this Dimension of Nothingness could be, which was called unattainable by others. Maybe it was at a distance I could reach... Those who were convinced that the forest was impassable had never tried to transcend it. Why would I give up without ever trying? Most prefer not to try at all instead of trying and failing. There is a chance of success in what has not been tried yet, and arrogance loves to set in this chance.

I had to make my own decision by trying it myself. Behind this forest would be the dimension of NOTHINGNESS, the Truth Dimension. How far you can see and think about what's ahead reveals the quality of the training you have had so far. If you can only think or create ideas about your home, your workplace and the living spaces of your city, then you are not looking at the future but only what's in front of you. Let's see how those here are doing about this...

How far does this forest go? What's the depth of it?

Nirvanian: We do not know. All we know is that it is impassable. Could the impossible have a distance? We would not go into the water of which we can't see the bottom, or head off on a road whose end we can't see.

(They did not have any guardians to protect against the dangers that might have come from the forest at night. As it did not disrupt their lives and their peace, they preferred not to regard the forest as a problem or a danger; they pretended as if it was not there at all. **If there was none that had come from beyond the forest or travelled further from here, then who were those that had persuaded the ones who told you that the forest was unreachable and that you should wait here?**

Nirvanian: We do not know who persuaded those who have told us. But that is what everyone knows and believes here! Here, those who know do not talk, and those who do not know talk a lot.

(They were trying to avoid my talking by indicating implicitly that I was talking too much. It was impossible to blame them. Their learned helplessness was evident and it prevented them to go any further, having almost turned into an unintentional attitude that was carried as a genetic heritage. Even the idea of departure was enough to make people feel strange and stressed, let alone entering the forest.

Yet when I expressed what I felt, they began to think that I was disturbing their peace. But I was not to be one of those who could not remember the path of truth because of the fear experienced as dealing with the problems encountered on the path.)

If those who know do not speak up, the stage is left to others who do not know. So people would believe in those who do not know but talk, and ignorance would rule the world. I believe that as those who really know speak, the others who do not know would first remain quiet with the joy of learning and speak when they are in the know. Haven't those who know learned in order to talk and teach in the first place?

Nirvanian: *Yes you are right. Only those who know should speak and those who do not know should learn before they speak.*

Those who know speak only when it is required to do so. A question comes up here, as to decide who knows and who doesn't.

(When I meet someone who excludes me or tries to exercise power on me, I do not consider the obstacles they create or the influence of these obstacles, I rather consider the fear in their heart because of lack of love. I do not allow their fear to contaminate me. On such occasions I recall what Genghis Khan said when he was confronted with the Great Wall of China which seemed insurmountable: **"The strength of this wall is as much as the heart of the man who built it."** *Those who focus on*

*the apparent problem cannot see the fear in the heart of the man who built the wall because they focus on the strength of the wall. Yet the man who built the wall has actually built it to hide his fear. Those who reject new knowledge are generally afraid of it as they do not know what they will become if they receive it. What is old is the enemy of the new. We should gently take them to future by meeting their tough respond with love and understanding through illuminating their fears. Seeking new answers is like leaving the house on a dark night and entering a deserted and dark forest. Yet, as Victor Huge said, "**No army can resist the power of a thought whose time has come.**" Everyone may lose his way, and this is when it becomes crucial who or what he accepts as a guide.*

I felt a sudden optimism and my body was almost recharged with energy. When I said "I have had enough rest and food. The seeker of Truth has the right to rest but he has no right to turn back on his path. I would like to continue and go into the forest", most of them looked puzzled and said "We guess you want to commit suicide". The principle which suggests 'stable structures influence unstable structures" worked there as well. A few indecisive people who wished to rekindle the flame of quest in them said "we are coming too" which caused greater puzzlement in others. We gathered together to set off on the unknown paths of the fatal forest feeling reignited and revived with the hope of becoming 'those who know'. When an old man beside me noticed that I was looking at the innkeeper and those left behind with a slight humiliation, he said "Why are you looking down on those left behind?".

THE GURUS AROUND US AND
ENERGY LEVELS

I am looking at those who have lost their self-confidence and their sense of adventure, who are waving at those heading forward, and who will no longer be as happy and peaceful as they once were.

The Man: Do you notice that by only focusing on reaching the truth dimension, you regard any achievements in between as failures, and do not recognize how they contribute to you and to the whole. Wholeness is considered to be somewhere up above where everything is held together. Yet everything you experience is a wholeness in itself; your family, your class, your school, your team etc. For example, the Istanbul-Nirvana road that you took from Istanbul to Nirvana is a wholeness of a path with its rocks, soil, animals, roads, trees, inns and people. Each of those on the path is a part of the wholeness of your path.

If you only focus on reaching the Truth Dimension, you cannot see the value of what is on the way and you cannot receive what you really need. If there were no inns on the road, you would not be able to eat, rest, or know of those who have gone further before. Because their duty is to ensure that those who arrive can rest, to help those who will stay, turn back or go further without interfering with the free will of anyone. They are also responsible not to encourage anyone who cannot go further and avoid causing their death on the road. If life is a matter of evolution, then nothing animate/inanimate in your life has been created in vain. Each of them is a Guru for you.

Were this way and all the people on the way my gurus?

The Man: *Definitely... Evolution indicates a process, and Gurus are within the process. Gurus do not perform physical aesthetic surgeries like surgeons. You can't say, 'I have a little too much vanity, I'd like it to be removed! I don't have sufficient tolerance, I'd like to increase it.'*

Guru is the person who uses the ancient wisdom and universal truths to reveal the potential within the student. He shows you what you already have, he does not give birth to anything but he makes you give a birth. The Guru does not make the devotee take decisions; his duty is to support the devotee to find his own answers by enhancing the devotee's perception. The Guru shows who you are, he teaches you about yourself. In the dervish convents they would tell those who had become adepts "You are ready, you have nothing more to learn from us, go to Hasan Sezai Hodja and continue your initiation" or "Go to West and preach the teaching". Guru approaches to the disciple as if he has found a bird with an injured wing that cannot fly. He takes the bird, heals it and then sets it free.

Briefly, he trains his student to live a life where he determines his own rules and asks everything to himself. He does this by creating an emotional bond with the student, without interfering with the student's free will. He rescues, heals and sets free. As it is known that the greatest harm that could be done to a faith is to allow inadequate gurus preach it before they realize the initiation themselves, the students who have not reached the maturity to complete the initiation are not sent out into the public and rather used for the administrative affairs in the dervish convent.

In Summary: The Guru does not transform you into something else, he introduces you to yourself by helping you to discover your being.

You are absolutely right. Everyone searches for someone to show him what he has in himself. Everyone waits for someone that will tell them, "Come on, you can do it! I believe you will succeed." Yet, you should first believe in yourself. Who would believe you if you do not believe in yourself?

The Man: *So Guru is the person who sees and shows you what you already have but cannot see, he believes in you and makes you believe in yourself. As you mentioned, all you need is a little support sometimes, and the best support you can give someone might be convincing them that trying does not necessarily mean failing. Most people think that failing without having tried is a more honourable choice rather than trying and failing. Because they consider failing after trying as something to be ashamed of, as a failure. The guru should make his students feel that they cannot know if they can succeed or not without trying, rather than making them feel that 'they can do anything'.*

Imagine you have a son who is 15 and he asks your help for everything he can do on his own like drinking water, sitting on a chair or studying. What will you do? God says "Do something, make an effort so that I can support you. Yet you want me to do everything for you instead of making an effort" and does not answer the prayers that you say for the things you can do yourself. God expects you to say "Take care of me", not "Drive me".

Why aren't there any Gurus to preach these in today's world?

The Man: *If you need a humane Guru who constantly speaks to you, that means you couldn't discover your essence. You cannot imagine how much those who look for a human Guru miss by failing to see that anything around them could be a guru. The Creator imposes his Knowledge on us as 'evolution' through His reflections in those He created.*

People of all levels and everything in this world where even a leaf does not move without His permission, are your Gurus as being the reflections of the Creator. Just as each traveller, each innkeeper, each tree, each flower and this deadly forest is your guru... The logic is simple; **you are student of those who preach and the teacher of those who ask.**

Is the forest a Guru as well?

The Man: *Of course, Guru is the one who shows what is within you. He shows you what you can and what you cannot. Does this* *forest not bring out the fear or courage in people? Does it not show you what you really are? Are you aware? This forest which represents death, the impossible, the NOTHINGNESS, is challenging all who come here, by saying "Are you ready to go through?".*

Most people choose to answer this simple question by creating answers that turn this journey into a superhuman one that is 'impossible to pass', claiming "No one has been able to pass it, no one has even tried it. I would try if it was a forest that could be passed.", instead of admitting "Not me". Yet you can never stop those who have nothing to lose, those who have dedicated their lives to this quest, those whose desire is stronger than their fear, and whose mind and vision are nowhere but focused on the path. Because no hindrance can stand before those who seek love; words cannot scare them.

While this forest is a challenge for some, it is an invitation for others. If there is an invitation from what's ahead and you have felt this invitation, then it has shown you what you already have. This fatal forest and what's ahead of it seems impossible for everyone. It is an area which must first be illuminated and conquered. Remember, something that is designed for you cannot be more powerful or difficult than you. No one is given a load that he cannot carry and no obstacle is placed before anyone who cannot overcome it.

For those who do not receive this invitation, this is a fatal and dark area full of dangers. They will be upset and become worried for you, they will even try to stop you.

The Man: This situation reminds me of the relationship between a great person known to be enlightened, called Ali, son of Melikdad and his son Muhammad Şemseddinin (Hz. Şemsi Tebrizi): "I had not reached puberty then. I would not eat anything when I dove into the sea of love. I would have no need, I would endure the days of hunger and thirst. One day my father said to me: "My son, I cannot understand you, where will this end? This attitude will lead you to a tragedy" he said. And I answered:

Father! Do you know what our relationship is like as a father and son? Imagine they place a duck egg together with the chicken eggs under the chicken and the chicks hatch when the time comes. The chicks follow their mother all together and come to the side of a lake. The chick that came out of the duck egg immediately jumps into the water. The chicken who sees this starts to panic thinking that her baby is drowning. However the duckling swims happily. This is the difference between me and you. "

__The Man:__ Do you think it is right for the duck to encourage the chicks in vain and put them under risk?

Is it duck, or the chicken? I think you first have to jump into the water in order to understand. Some of those here just followed me without even thinking as I said "I am going". Does this not show that they were ready? Did I not show them what was within them?

Here is what Rumi says in a similar situation: "Your mother is the goose of the sea of Truth... Your heart's inclination for the sea and the nature of your heart come from your mother... If your nanny makes you scared of the water, do not fear and run towards the sea. You can live both in dry and in wet, that is to say both on the land and in the sea."

__The Man:__ Some of the people here were stuck between their past and their future, in the zone of waiting. They were the indecisive ones who cannot decide to go back or forward. They were just waiting for a sign in order to go forward. You have told them that it was the time to go. Maybe you convinced them just for your own interests.

What is this supposed to mean? Why would I interfere with their free will? I brought out what was within them. They were ready to burn, I was just their spark. I don't think I understand what you mean...

__The Man:__ Could it not be your yearning to find someone who *would ensure that you were not alone and help you forget about your fears of going forward? You say the innkeeper has stopped those here to take money from them and have them serve for him. Who is to say that you did not do the same to have them serve for you on the journey? In short, why do you care so much about these people you do not know?*

If I take those who cannot make the journey, I will slow down because of dealing with their demands of rest or water. You know that excitement is contagious. I just said I was going. I wanted them not to give up without trying. If they find the path challenging, they can return back to their safe inn.

As the road is long and there are many issues to deal with, you get tired of struggling with problems being exhausted. Isn't it smart to give up without spoiling your charisma, by even proclaiming the journey as a story of success and declaring that the Truth Dimension is unreachable? They were suddenly awakened when I reminded them that they had just stopped. Furthermore, who is to say that the forest does not end just over the next hill if no one knows how far it is. When they responded 'yes, why not', they reclaimed the courage inflicted on them by the historical blockages and told me that they were ready. Those who stayed at Nirvana had low energy, what could I do for them?

The Man: *Did you like your primary school teacher?*

A lot. Confucius says "The greatest fortune is to have good teachers during the childhood." My Teacher Sevim has been the person who enabled me to arrive where I am, she has been very influential in building a solid foundation on my path.

The Man: Was she a person with a low energy, low consciousness and a low frequency just because she was a primary level teacher?

Not at all, she and my other teachers were all fantastic teachers. Sevim who was my class teacher was the best. I have been most lucky to have good and wise teachers like her, during my middle school, high school and later education years as well. Not only in school though, my grandparents, my mother and aunts were very wise people too.

I saw my mistake in classifying people and I was embarrassed.

The Man: There is no level in this learning process. No one is less worthy than the other, because each and every one becomes a very important part of your process. You would not be here if your primary school teacher was not good. Primary school was very difficult when you were there. And when you were in middle school, primary school was easy while middle school was difficult. Including high school and university levels, each was easier compared to a higher level yet none of them can exist without the former. Each one is hard in itself, but they are all a part of the learning process. Now when you look back, which one is a low level?

None?

The Man: *Do you see? They are all equally important. Think of it this way, what would have happened if you had directly arrived at Nirvana Inn? What kind of a person would you be?*

I would be exactly like those born here. I may not have found the courage to enter the forest because I would not have overcome the challenging journey before.

The Man: *And that is the importance of the process. Do you know what a vaccine is? It is injecting a small amount of the microbe into the body to increase strength of the immunity against a possible illness so that the body is introduced to the disease and learns to fight. When the day comes and the disease pathogens are transmitted in a higher dose, the body fights with the disease as it learned as a result of the vaccine. The hunger, thirst, the sleeplessness, the uncertainties and the discouraging words on the way to Nirvana were also a kind of spiritual vaccine. They were the spiritual vaccines that prepared you for a harder fight, for this forest.*

So you say the pain that does not kill you just makes you stronger both physically and spiritually!

The Man: *Exactly. You must consider the assessments of energy, dimension or frequency as a journey consisting of horizontal* *regions instead of vertical levels. Just like this Road from İstanbul to Truth. Each exists to prepare you for the next stage, and one's worth is never less or more than another. Each exists to prepare you for the next condition as being specialized in different areas of your learning process. The place you interpret as 'giving up', the place where the traveller understands he cannot go any further, is the point where the person finds himself in the picture of the whole. That is the place where he will help those who come there. He may stop temporarily, and set off again after a while.*

Caring the process will enable you to notice that everything animate or inanimate around you is either a Guru and a student. You will let go of the vertical viewpoint which discerns a lower or higher and ruins the reverence for the parts of the process. This viewpoint causes us to devalue and underestimate the people in our lives. Someone who does not know as much as you do or more than you do cannot be considered as low-level in the Golden Age of Knowledge. The Golden Age of Knowledge is an era where every type of knowledge is very important. The humans will build a new relationship with the universe and everything in it, they will experience a new level of integrity. All the processes are the tests for you to protect your Personal Integrity as well.

Personal integrity?

The Man: *What happened? You are surprised. Yes, Personal Integrity, your own individual wholeness. One should establish his* *own original character around his essence, and attain a unity between his thoughts and actions. He will have a split personality and his integrity will be fragmented unless he does so. This is called Mandala (Circle) or wholeness in Far East. One should first establish his own integrity. The family, neighbourhood, city, country, organization, religion, race are each a wholeness. The highest wholeness in the world dimension is humanity and all the animate/inanimate beings. One who finds his centre reaches the wholeness and the unity of the humanity and becomes a perfect human. Being perfect does not grant a state of being above others; it is being fair and modest without losing faith.*

If the difficulties you experienced or the people you met coming to Nirvana had made you lose your belief and determination, you would not have preserved your personal integrity and become weak, so you could not have gone beyond Nirvana. What you experienced on the way enhanced your Personal Integrity. When you reached the deadly forest, the peaceful and happy environment of Nirvana could not stop you.

It is very important how one interprets what he lives. Those who see their experiences as a penalty and a source of suffering put themselves under stress lower their own energy. They wear out quickly and it is not only their souls, but also their physical bodies that become worn out. Their veins narrow down. Those who consider their experiences as a spiritual vaccine, an endurance test, a source of stress which increases their spiritual condition enhance their physical health as well. You determine your spiritual and physical life

quality depending on how you view the half-empty glass. What do you say for those who give up not being able to stand the challenges, and commit suicide?

The Man: *The soul becomes a murderer by killing the body in a suicide. For this reason, they are punished in the abode of souls. They get recorded in the Collective Memory as individuals who have given up not being able to deal with the challenges.*

Many people are unaware that they use a long term suicide method by using cigarettes, alcohol, drugs etc.

Where is faith in this system?

The Man: *We had said "We were inspired by God, and made it for humanity". In fact, most of us call this dimension the Divine Knowledge Dimension. This stage is where faith is renewed with science and technology. Divine love leads to the revealing of the divine mystery. The love of truth is the love of searching, finding and knowing which knows no obstacles. Obstacles cannot stand before the Love of Truth, words cannot scare it. Love is not being attached to the particle or dominating the particle. It is not imprisoning the particle while being imprisoned by it. Everyone wants to find their own place, and cannot stand to stay anywhere until they find it. Love is overcoming the possibility of being possessed by a particle or a material but reaching the divine limit through it. One sometimes thinks he has found it and stops, yet understands after a while of rest that this is not his place. So he heads off again. The unknown sea of NOTHINGNESS which is said to be impossible is a sea of love that only lovers can pass. As Yunus said, "Any place where there is love is heaven, and any heart which love does not reside is the hell."*

Why is sacrifice essential?

The Man: *Think of this way, as you can give up something like a match, candle, fire, torch or an electric lamp, the darkness turns into light. Once you put out the light, it is dark again. The more space you want to illuminate for a longer time, the more matches, candles, wood, batteries, electricity you need to give up. If you only think of the match, candle, wood, battery, electricity when we say 'sacrifice', then you will focus on the material things you can replace. The true sacrifice you make is the time which you cannot replace and the hope that gives you the competence to illuminate.*

My love of truth and my faith is the star in the sky that shows me the way. I am a traveller on behalf of the all travellers for the good of the whole.

The Man: *This is a journey from yourself to yourself. You see, you are the path, and the traveller as well. The day you understand this you are in the Truth Dimension and you are then the Truth Itself.*

The Truth dimension, the place where all questions and answers are found!

The Man: *You are right but the truth dimension is a circle of* *knowledge which continually expands, like the NOTHINGNESS dimension. As you reach the limits of one, you realize a higher dimension of truth. The higher dimension is the one that contains all the questions and answers of the level you are found in. So you always want to reach the Truth Dimension that has the questions and answers of the next level. A previous Truth Dimension you leave behind does not mean much to you any more, it becomes a former truth dimension.*

(It is hard to believe but after a few hills and a few plains, we reached the end of the forest that was said to be impassable. We reached a plain covered with tall green grass and the record ended. I asked to Heaven "Why did the record end? I had learned the NOTHINGNESS Dimension in my previous Dreamcarnation but why couldn't I remember it here?".)

Heaven: *Fear exists to bring out the courage. What counted was to take the decision to enter the forest and do it, taking the step into the fatal forest which scares one to death. Think of yourself as an actor; you become a different character in each movie. Yet none of them is your original essence. They each leave something in your mind and can enter into the depths of your heart and settle in your essence. In Thinkmatic the short term memory is reset during the transition between the dreams. But the attributes which have taken their place in your original memory having turned into intellectual reflexes are not disturbed. The fatal forest of centuries ago manifests as the fatal space in this era. The achievements which have been left in your essence by your experiences at the boundaries of the forest and in the forest* *come out of your subconscious as reactive behaviours, and you see the open invitation that calls from the NOTHINGNESS dimension beyond the space. Then all your effort is to transcend the space. You know that your happiness is beyond the space. Your new forest is the fatal SPACE that is impossible to transcend.*

Watching myself, especially my successful self was very good. 'Is that all? We just came to the most exciting part.'

Heaven: The truth seeker is the one who can take a step towards the unknown in order to find his very essence, at the point where everyone stops and says there is no further. He does not take the easy way out and surrender to the circumstances, he rather does all he can, and waits patiently. Will he take the shape of the container he enters in, or give his own shape to the container? This is the most important aspect we consider. Hz. Akşemseddin said to his student, Fatih Sultan Mehmet "If you do not surrender to any circumstances, work hard and preserve your faith, then the circumstances will change and surrender to you." Years later, Fatih Sultan Mehmet would say "If they are smart enough to chain the Straits, then we are crazy enough to transport the ships over the land." and conquered Istanbul by transporting the ships over the land. What was the hardest thing for you on the road, and what made you continue at that point?

"Not giving up without trying." Why should this forest, which others have claimed to be fatal and limitless and declared impassable without trying, be my obstacle? Not hav-

ing tried before was what has made me set off. The greatest disadvantage of those people who have not achieved while they could is the lack of the people who believe in them. Not only there was not anyone on the way that would encourage, but also there were many who made statements such as "What you travelled so far is not even a patch on the rest of the path.", "You are wasting your life on a rumour which is not real", "Stay here, live in peace and happiness with wealth" etc. It is a real test of willpower for those who do not have a sufficient level of faith in themselves...

Heaven: Remember that we first eliminated your emotional obstacles. They were the internal hindrances in your brain. There are also people you met outside, 'the blockage people' we send. If you have no intention to go further, you use them as a pretext to go back and live a happy and peaceful life. You should take them seriously and decide wisely whether their advice is sensible or not. You must pay attention to those people who might stop you through giving unreasonable advice, or those who can throw you in danger by imposing a futile encouragement. You should stay away from those who give you unhealthy advice.

What do you think of the scenario of reaching Nirvana which we designed to assess the limits and the material and spiritual persistence of a person?

The richness of the Nirvana Inn draws you in with its peaceful environment, being located at the borders of the fatal forest which is reached after all the physical and spiritual difficulties at a point where no one considers taking a step forward. Watching such hard lessons which one has learned but does not remember is indeed a very uplifting and useful form of training. Thank you very much.

Heaven: What is the most crucial lesson that you learned?

Peace alone is not enough for happiness. If you are not happy, it indicates that you are not using your essential energy (essential power), and you do not trust your intuition. It applies for your love life as well; you cannot express and experience your love if you are unhappy. Being unhappy in professional life indicates that you cannot utilize your talents fully. In short, if you are unhappy then you have a blockage which means that you have stopped to actualize yourself. You cannot shine brightly unless you do not fulfil what you were born to manifest.

Heaven: Those who relate their unhappiness to others are the ones who relate to others to be happy as well. Thinkmatic, is the fight between knowing who you are in essence, and telling who you really are. Those who remain indecisive in this fight, become attached to something more decisive and more powerful, and follow their rule. Being told what to do for a long time makes you lose the courage and desire to do anything on your own, you end up doing only what you are told. A dictatorship called Family Democracy was developed taking advantage of those indecisive and aimless people's inclination to avoid responsibility. The governing systems of the countries and the ti-

tles of the administrators (Father/Brother etc.) were planned ac-cordingly.

*First seen in Indonesia, this "one person rule" or dictatorship was called "Guided Democracy" or "Family Democracy" by Sakurna, in which he was the "Father". (It reminds of Demirel who was called Father) In time this **Family Democracy"** was accepted by most of Indonesians; they were comfortable about "leaving everything to the Father". Leaving the decisions up to others avoids you to blame as well as being blamed by others.*

Statements such as 'Having travelled for centuries, we are still at the beginning of the path'. or 'What we know is nothing compared to what we need to learn.' are actually confessions related to the failure of the teaching. They name it progress when it is only 'circumambulation of an idea'. Believing in false forms of 'wholeness' which were introduced by taking advantage of the people's yearning to be part of a whole, causes mental blindness.

Meanwhile you think you are surrendering to Family Democracy in the name of a good cause, for the sake of the whole. When the occupation is completed, you end up doing everything you are told, including your daily choices, and 'the wholeness of thoughts' starts to rule your material life. One who takes over your soul controls your material world, and he who takes over your material world controls your soul.

*Think of what your current job and your current environment brings out or improves in you. Understand how you can be more beneficial for the real whole and do your best with great love. **What you need to know about the real power within you is that new questions and small acts can lead to great changes in your life.** So, what do you say about space, which corresponds to the fatal forest of that century?*

It is an impossible emptiness consisting of impossible distances and living conditions for the physical human body or his nafs. What's beyond the space is the Truth Dimension, where there is an answer for everything. When you free yourself from the nafs and see through the eyes of your soul, space is nothing but a three dimensional recording device, somewhere that contains all the answers being called as Collective Memory, Divine Archive, Cosmic Memory, Union Store, Lawh-i Mahfuz etc. Thus space is not an obstacle which must be overcome in body, but a system which must be solved mentally. Answers are not beyond the space, they are within the space.

Heaven: I congratulate you. You got the idea of freeing yourself from your nafs and overcoming it. In addition to its literal meaning, each word has also a philosophical meaning which it borrows from its past and that is actually the true meaning of that word. When you look with your heart's eye and understand the essence of the obstacles, challenges or the unknown, then you can be free of the prejudices, obsessions or fears created by the literal meanings. By this way you reach the essential knowledge. As you discover the essential knowledge, any obstacle, challenge or absence turn into an answer. At this very moment when the whole universe fits into a human heart, one no longer stays as an ordinary person but he becomes a special person that can see what everything that happens corresponds to in the truth dimension, just like Rumi, Socrates, Yunus, Plato, Hadgi Bektash, Shems-i Tebrizi. Do you notice that space also fulfils the human's need for the sense of eternity!

How?

Heaven: No one wants to be forgotten or adopt a creation scenario that ends with being completely forgotten. The belief in God fulfils people's need for a sense of eternity. No one follows a life model which ends with an earthly body and ignores the soul. The Collective Memory will remain in space as long as the space exists. The life records satisfy humans' need for the sense of eternity and their desire not to be forgotten.

So some harder material and spiritual problems and poverty are waiting for me.

***Heaven:** You are wrong, we are not only tried with poverty but also with abundance. It's another way of really getting to know someone to give him a status and grant him power. We want to train them as people who can endure poverty and hardship as well as begin able to manage power and wealth.*

How do you determine the subject and the content of the training in Thinkmatic?

Heaven:** Imagine you are given a task of establishing a school where education of any level in every field is provided. We determine following the starting criteria as to determine which training will be given in what subject at what level (primary school, middle school, college / regular, occupational, engineering, fine arts, media, sports etc.). Briefly, it's the **Needs** and **Talents!

If you have no chance of sending astronauts into space, it will be pointless to establish a space base or a launch pad, and give space training to people at school. You only create simulations in those areas that you require in the real world. It is like establishing plane simulations for the training of the pilots when you travel by airplanes in real life. Departments are launched to offer the trainings for those subjects that you need in reality. When it comes to talent, I have to make use of any talent and open a department for each. If there is someone with a talent for weightlifting then I have to establish a weightlifting hall and find a coach to give him the opportunity to succeed. You see, every-

one is here on earth in order to prepare for a mission that's of a higher level than the worldly dimension.

What do you think is the most important benefit of simulation?

Heaven: *If you remember, we mentioned about divine technology. The divine aspect of simulation is giving the opportunity to try unlimitedly in a desired condition and time. You don't entrust an airplane to a novice pilot in any weather condition. In this case, you should wait for the rain and snow to fall, and the wind to blow in order to be able to test the pilot in rainy, snowy or windy weather. You also need to wait until the candidate pilot and the instructor are ready as well when the necessary conditions occur. The most important aspect of simulation is its ability to create artificial conditions like rain, storms, snow etc. and provide opportunities for training without putting the student or the instructor at risk.*

In fact, much more has been achieved in many areas. The earthquake tests for a building to be constructed and the wind tunnel tests for a planned airplane is performed directly by the computer. It is assessed whether the design of the building or the airplane is appropriate and only then the manufacturing is commenced. The airplanes whose prototype has been made is only produced after it is tested in wind tunnels against all wind/storm conditions it can possibly encounter.

You have set the stage in Thinkmatic and people are competing within the scenarios. So how is the achievement measured and assessed?

Heaven: Selecting a first place has always reinforced the level of success in education. The person who can perform and reveal his potential better is rewarded. As there are no competitors but only you in Dreammatic, you are in your most natural state whereas there are competitors and figures that provoke you in Thinkmatic. The most critical factor that affects the success of the system in both of them is your evaluation that is fair enough not to encounter any objection.

Those who watch the videos will make the decisions easily. No one can object if everything is recorded.

Heaven: You forget the humane factors! There is a saying "If you really want to get to know someone, give him a status". When people gain a position and notice they can have anything they want, their ambitions and emotions that have been suppressed may come out of control and take over the individuals. A person we have known for years may become someone completely different making life unbearable for themselves and those around them. We call this situation where power seduces people 'the God Complex'. It is a shock or an intoxication of power which turns one into a monster that thinks everyone should bear with him (he believes that he can do anything to them and have them do anything for him. This occurs when one believes he is indispensable). So, let me explain this through a scenario of abundance used in Thinkmatic:

You are a manager in a factory. The chief who is responsible for ten people in one of your departments retires. You have to select a new chief. However, none of them has the experience the chief has and you cannot estimate how they might treat the workers when they become a chief. How do you tackle with this issue of promotion? Who do you select as the chief and what criteria do you use?

I would select the best worker after comparing their former performances, and make him the chief temporarily. I would establish an observation team of one or two workers who work with him constantly to give me information so that I can be aware of everything he does. I can easily assess the success of the department he manages by analysing the production. He can't even make a move without my knowing, as I establish a control system.

Heaven: *The methods have aspects which relieve people, yet they also possess human flaws. The success depends on the people that act in between. That's to say:*

How was the relationship of these people who will provide you information with the new chief in the past? Were there any personal problems between them such as animosity, envy, competition? How much can you trust the information given to you by someone who is aware that he can very much influence your decisions? How do you know that he will not use you as a pawn for his personal problems with the chief by giving you incorrect information? How do you guarantee that the person who is second in line for being a chief will not think "His failure will pave the way for me", and hinder the work by influencing others negatively?

I will not have one person, I can figure out the true information by having two or three of them.

Heaven: *What will you do when the results you obtain from different people are contradictory? How can you be sure that the workers do not recognize your informants and behave differently when they are around? How will you know that they do not exercise financial and spiritual pressure on those under their command by insulting them and putting them under stress? They may even give harm to their family lives. How will you ensure that those people help you aren't considered as 'snitchers'? How will you alleviate the emotional pressure they experience? Most important of all, will you be able to identify such a situation before things get out of hand?*

When they are not successful and you say "I have to remove you from the position of chief, because you have been unsuccessful", and he say, "OK but 2-3 workers on my team are not working properly due to personal problems with me, they did their best for me to be unsuccessful" etc. will the situation not become more complicated? When you appoint someone new in their place as chief and demote them to their old position, how will you ever resolve the trauma of failure you have created due to your incorrect decision. Do you think he can be an efficient worker, or even more, a happy person like he was before? Maybe he was just experiencing a bad period and you should have been more understanding towards him, and help him to use his opportunity better? Do you see where you got to with just what you did regarding just one of the tens of chiefs under your rule. Your chief appointment decision which can seem very simple to you is considered together with families, see how must it has positively or negatively affected the lives of hundreds of people.

Abundance is as difficult as poverty and we do not realize it? Or even more difficult, because we are responsible for others with the decisions we make. While making decisions which may seem simple, your own private life must also be very healthy. You must be resistant in the face of material/spiritual problems, and you must not be affected by the emotional turmoil of the people you rule by these decisions.

Heaven: *As you can see, your decision can be easily affected by the human factors we call the five passions (Anger, Greed, Lust, Material Dependence, Arrogance). As you said, maybe there* *was a problem in the private life of that person during that period, and maybe he could not succeed in being a very successful chief because he could not focus sufficiently. Let us consider the chief who really is bad; you entrust a chief who with a decision taken in the testing process and with the methods applied, has damaged the private lives of 10 workers.*

Then consider this for positions which involve more people, with much harsher and fatal consequences, such as Mayor, Minister, Prime Minister etc. How do you explain effecting the quality of life of everyone living in a city with a decision, a decision where thousands of people lose their jobs, cannot pay their instalments, where children have to be removed from school, where they lose their homes, where in short their lives become destroyed?

How does God allow this? How does He allow one to have a deep impact on the lives of others? Does God love one more than the other, that he is just an onlooker in their lives being affected so much? Now do you understand the importance of Thinkmatic simulation? We do not place people in office and entrust real people without trying anyone sufficiently with the illusion events and people in the simulation. Everyone in the Thinkmatic, take serious tests regarding their behaviour towards the people entrusted to them, work and ideas. The injustice due to partisanship, same city, same association, relation ties are not in question with us. Let me just emphasize this subject with an example from a book by Vehbi Koç: "A person appointed with influence is like a gifted cockerel. You can't slaughter it, it doesn't give eggs, you just keep feeding it." States, workplaces, factories which will their staff with gifted cockerels are doomed to fail.

No matter what, if there is a need for a chief, these trials and those that are hurt will exist unfortunately. Everything has a reason. I believe in the Creator's divine justice.

Heaven: *We also believe in Divine Justice, however are there not times when only belief is not sufficient, and we must do something too? Of course there is no problem for those that are well-to-do, however for those looking in, these difficulties, they are each a process which they must experience for the evolution of others. They even requested this themselves with their thoughts, and the universe met their requests. Sometimes we hear defences such as "I gave him the opportunity to be Chief, but he didn't use it". Well, did you ever consider that you may be a factory manager who made the decision to make the wrong person chief? Or instead of thinking like this, does it comfort you enough to say* **it happened because he wanted it.** *Maybe the one tested is not just the chief, but you who made the deci-sion of the chief. Who knows, maybe only you...*

So many criteria, possibilities and decisions which affect so many people. A very good example of how a factory manag-er who only looks to results and who is not interested in the process can make work complicated. When making decisions regarding people, you must make a decision realizing that it can change the lives of not just one person but hundreds of people, education is a must!

Heaven: *You are so right. If you wish to work with good factory managers, good chiefs, good workers, then you must select the teaching staff at schools very carefully. Thick of students who have been educated by inexperienced teachers with inadequate, incomplete information. The teacher, in order to cover up their own failure, gives high grades and undeserving graduates, the insufficiency which seems small, has a butterfly effect on the lives of the children, and will become a load they will have to carry for the rest of their lives. Their professional inadequacies will affect their families, the people they live with and all people affected by the decisions they make. Different regions, different schools, different teachers and different results. There is a standard curriculum in education, but if the standard of knowledge and teaching is not the same in teachers, are children not going to be raised in an unjust environment? Those that compensate for this will be successful and those who don't will live its problems for a lifetime.*

So how does the Thinkmatic select the ideal chief?

Heaven: *The most just choice is the case where all ten workers are given the chance of being chief and where no one is damaged by these trials. Trial you do not know which one would be better than the chef. Even the person himself, not for the opportunity given, may not be aware of the chief of the store. Because as the environment where he can show his talents as chief have not been created, he is unaware of the successful chief within him. From the memory records of the workers in the department where the chief will be, an illusion copy of that department of the factory is created, and loaded in the Thinkmatic. Then, the factory workers of each individual chef illusion you do in that section. Each are tested one at a time according to scenarios prepared for tens, hundreds of possibilities, and you complete the best chief selection with success. And this "Equal Opportunity" as you do deliver. All ten of the workers were given the same opportunity, each were given the opportunity to show themselves, and the chief was selected in such a way as there can be no objection.*

Even the existence in the group of someone who says if I was given the chance I would have done better will lead to problems in the group in time. Judicious choice when will respect the right of everyone to the new chief conductor of winning and will obey.

What are the main criteria in this scenario?

Heaven: *You can find them yourself. Workplace, you will be able to choose a chief business and personnel safety, what do you care?*

Diligence, not providing benefits to themselves or those he is close to. Giving permits to those they know, giving easier tasks, employing those close to him, anger management, information control, patience control, alcohol, night life, reticence etc, they are what come to my mind at first.

Heaven: Work also varies according to the details of these general criteria.

Did you not give any clue to these unknowing people who were unaware they were being tested?

*Heaven: The biggest clue is their conscience. One that sounds enough conscience will understand what to do when you use the mind. **Reason** and **conscience**, this pair are very important. If you listen to only your conscience, you will believe that everyone who is crying right, innocent, or loves a lot.*

At the beginning of this section you said that the criteria of the school is determined by the needs and talents, what is the situation in terms of talent?

Heaven: How do you know what a child is talented in?

I will try them in all areas, sports, theatre, dance, art, music, cinema, sculpture etc. They will continue with whichever one they are successful in.

Heaven: You said sport. Which branch? Basketball, volleyball, handball, football, athletics, fencing, archery, boxing, karate, cycling, ice skating? How will you know which you are most talented in without trying them all like swimming, wrestling, weightlifting, judo, kayaking, boating, climbing, tennis, squash, under water, sailing, golf, gymnastics, riding etc.?

As there are tens of branches in art, due to limited time I will be limited to a few trials. By reaching a general conclusion with a few trials we will continue with an average decision.

__Heaven:__ In an even more difficult decision, what training will they receive and what will the real profession be: consider professions such as engineer, civil servant, worker, boss, doctor, fire fighter, refuse collector, lawyer, police officer, soldier, bureaucrat, grocer, florist,

banker, physicist, chemist, economist, journalist, producer, presenter, printer, nurse, doorman, writer, shoemaker, mechanic, midwife, nurse, clergy, switchboard operator, doctor etc. What must be chosen for this child? How soon can you understand the accuracy or inaccuracy of the selection? How many children can try this profession?

Unfortunately generally one or two. Whether the choice of profession is right or wrong is clear when school is finished and you enter work and become the practitioner in real life. People switch to professions that are suited to them within a few years.

Heaven: *Unfortunately, people understood and passing of doing business after losing about 8-10 years. Also if there is a need for personnel in the profession they wish to change to or if the financial means of the person is suitable, then they have the opportunity to change. Does not work that had to endure a lot of people do not like? The purpose of student placement test is done on the elections which would be given to whom education Where? The success, graduates can be measured by whether they continue in their industry.*

You see, in the professions and skills in the world of elections size, is experiencing a very low system performance. What did we say before? Thinkmatic, trial offers unlimited possibilities for the identification of talent. The Thinkmatic offers the opportunity to measure talent in every branch of sports within minutes with illusion scenarios at the speed of light. So everyone the ability to appropriate, is directed to the sport will be the best.

With simulation scenarios regarding professions in the same way, within minutes the most suitable professions for people can be found by carrying out all training, practical training regarding any profession within minutes. Recruitment exams are not held at certain centres, anyone who wishes to can at any time, from anywhere connect to the Thinkmatic and test themselves with simulations at any level in any subject such as sports, art, profession and so on. After all, if you have never tried you cannot know if you have talent or not. Because the natural talent in their essence, when you see someone doing or trying it, you will say "That is what I want to do". An example on a world scale for this to be more clear: How do you organize a worldwide chess tournament?

Very easy, those who are winners in their own country will be called, they will all play against each other, and the winner is first.

Heaven: Let's think of it like this. Was everyone able to attend the qualifying in their own countries? Maybe some of them didn't even know. Only those who are members of specific chess clubs became aware, and screening was carried out among those who had already reached a certain level. Open to everyone, as you see, was not a competition that everyone can participate. There will be those who cannot take part in the screening because they have no money, because it is not convenient, because their health is not suitable that day, or those who fail the screening because of an issue in their private lives that day. Briefly, at the right time to pass the screening, at the right place and needs to be healthy. One chance, one attempt.

Whereas if we had held the qualifications of the competition online with a chess tournament, in a period of approximately 6 months, we gave everyone who wanted to the opportunity to joint the game and play as much as they like. How would it be if those at a certain level in the game of chess around the world were determined and their transport and accommodation costs met, and a final face to face competition was held? Qualification passed the screening of his machine, grab the right to play with real people.

It would be a very fair qualifying, and no one can make up excuses such as I was unlucky that day, I was not well, I had work to do. Everyone will be given a chance and called him the opportunity to demonstrate the ability of the unheard.

The Thinkmatic gives people the opportunity to show themselves with the three dimensional scenarios in the talents, professions etc. we listed below, time and time again. The most important difference, why does not know it's there, moving self-awareness. Not for anyone making the choice for him.

But Thinkmatic in the family, environment, and they do have those people to print.

Heaven: Think of it as the innkeeper and his friends on the way to them the way to Nirvana. Moving the centre of wisdom to measure your determination, without their awareness of extras. You get them, you think, but do not look for looks, you think you hear but do not hear. They are like remote-controlled puppet, just act according to the command received. Thinkmatic all those evolutionary conditioning your bearings, so Download the mix. If he's for your evolution, and you're there for her evolution. Centre of intellect, you are evolving together.

As you can see, it will be said to anyone who wishes to work in a certain area, sports, art, go and get a qualifying grade from the Thinkmatic and come back. They want those who can not come to a certain stage of the scenario in Thinkmatic not even get a job.

Thinkmatic, the future will be like the Human Resources Management System. Right, but when the memory of someone who has been successful in this is added to their memory, aren't the required characteristics reached directly?

Heaven: Good question. But our goal is to steer the direction of natural talent everyone. As you also upload information into memory, we can make knowledgeable, but the body and soul may be correspondingly. Think or it like this, everyone who goes to the same school, same class and takes the same lessons from the same teacher has the same raw information, but it has a different effect on each of them. If we instil instead of raw information interpreted information in all of them, then we will have removed their right to interpret the information with the information in their very essence. They are informed but unhappy. By copying his memory to you, we would be trying to make you, him. However our goal is to make you, you. Everyone should experience natural development in their natural talent. They

*must marry the right person, and have children when they are
ready!*

So really, not even getting married and having children goes through the Thinkmatic?

Heaven: *If nuclear families in society fall apart, then society it-self is irreversibly broken. The way to protect nuclear families is for suitable people to find each other and start families. Couples who believe they are suited for each other, must pass through possible marriage simulations in the Thinkmatic in order to get married. Couples who have been brought together unaware of where or why they are there, can be based upon scenarios in the Thinkmatic, and if they are still together then they are given permission to marry. In the same way as the importance of a happy family is known in children being good people, those who wish to have children will be mother/father in the Thinkmatic and will be tested with various scenarios regarding children and if they pass they will be able to have children. And they have to do this separately for each child. If there is a better way of measuring, why should society take the risk?*

If you wish let us continue with an example from the old world dimension where most are unaware of their talents, and the abil-ities of the Thinkmatic can be better understood. First of all abilities and the effects of the ability of individuals to life, so let's explain the breaking point. Did the tests or controls given to the apprentice given the forgotten money test in order to test the apprentice of the father end?

They were continually monitored at regular intervals in different ways.

Heaven: In fact, anyone who has something to do over again, they have to entrust similar tests at every stage. The health report, good conduct report, reference letters from previous workplaces, special tests requested according to the organization applied to, interviews etc. controls, are the efforts to get to know the people who will be employed and entrusted with something.

Does a mortal have the chance to understand and test the applied justice of the immortal, or the perfect the imperfect? How can the justice of the Thinkmatic be measured?

There are a lot of things that happened to me which I do not think I deserve at all. I comfort myself by saying that the Creator knows something, and I await him with peaceful curiosity, experiencing complete surrender to Him, but it is not at all easy. Was it too hard? (He starts to speak with a bit of laughter.)

Heaven: Wait calm down! The temperature has peaked again. As in some days in the Thinkmatic, you are heading off at full throttle again. When you are watching your past records in the future you will laugh at this.

Has the system not given up on you when it sends you instead of to the Fearmatic, to the Dreammatic, where everything is as you desire, where you never use the talents you have developed on earth and where you will live for eternity? In short, if you go to the Dreammatic or the Fearmatic, then it is like they have given up on you.

You are describing the greatest problem affecting the success of those living in the Thinkmatic, the problem of interpreting what they actually live, particularly the most painful? Most people who suffer a bad experience look to their own past and make an evaluation of the past which puts them in a good light, objecting with "What did I ever do to deserve this punishment? This punishment is clearly unfair".

Think of the children, while at certain times pox, mumps, hepatitis etc. can be fatal, sometimes they will catch diseases which can leave permanent damage. Or what would you do if you were to go to a country with an epidemic and there was a possibility you would be exposed? Of course, like your children you have a vaccine, or in other words you have to give a small amount of controlled microbes related to possible diseases, and teach your body to fight it. In the Thinkmatic, by giving controlled emotional vaccines in order to accustom the human soul to pain that will be experienced in the future or to measure their endurance or breaking point, sometimes we prepare them, and sometimes we test them. For this reason, when interpreting what you have experienced, think not only of the past but of the future, and always be honest so as to have free will to make such an assessment. Do not leave things in your past that can hold you back.

Honesty and freedom is very interesting. To be honest, liber-

ates people, can we elaborate on that?

Heaven: *When you are an honest person, because you do not have feelings of guilt you see things as they are and are free to interpret life. Subconscious feelings of guilt always leaves behind fear of punishment, and stops you from enjoying the day and looking to the future with hope. You must look forward to proceed. Those who look to the past and past information constantly, are like old souls in young bodies.*

In short, you say, "The pain I am experiencing is the result of an error in my past or the cost of happiness in my future".

Heaven: *What you live in a digital illusion, are spiritual experience. All of the Dreammatic, and almost all of the Thinkmatic, are no more than illusion puppets which act according to the commands received form the Central Brain. In reality you have not actually hurt anyone, however much you are responsible for what you have done in your dreams, you are that responsible here, there is no pain, and there is no happiness. Have you got the other one in a dream real? When she woke up in what you see in the dream they just remember the same dream? When a loved one you die in your dreams, you get upset when you wake up? "Thank God was a dream," he says, you appreciate a well. Dream no matter the initial criteria. As soon as you begin to see, you will continue as always was there. In Thinkmatic You can issue the initial criteria.*

How So?

Heaven: *When everything is as desired in the Dreammatic, mankind does not say "Why me?", whereas when something bad happens in the Thinkmatic, they object to Divine Justice, or fate, which means measure or appraised, with arabesque references such as "Why me", "What did I do to deserve this", "Is this your justice, world?".*

For their failures or sadness, they cling to rebellious questions such as "If you weren't going to care for it why did you have it? Why am I in this family, why am I in this country, why am I in this age? with **Starting Criteria.** *Without realizing it when they say "These conditions are too hard for me. I cannot do it, I cannot handle it, It is too hard" when they are attacking and blaming starting justice, only starting justice, they are asking for help from those around them, and mostly take refuge in material excuses such as "If I had been born in so and so country instead of this country, with its opportunities, if I had that car, that home, that family, look and see what I would have done?"*

Instead of attributing their happiness to material or the conditions of others in general and complaining about the existing conditions, by saying did I choose these conditions or are these the conditions offered to me, I don't know, but if there are my conditions, let's see what can be done with them, a mankind which does not surrender to conditions, has at their essence found divine power and started to use it for the benefit of the whole. As a thinker "a darkness that will complain candle!" You can think of Thinkmatic as rule being given to you to get to know you.

A Virtual God who "Gives to Take", who gives the earth and the sky to my command.

Heaven: The Thinkmatic is, at the end of a day, an illusion machine which produces starting scenarios according to specified rules and which face you with determined scenarios according to your choices. The decision maker and practitioner.

GIVING TO TAKE

We can call it a fair judge.

*Heaven: We can say it is the fairest of judges. The preparation of the rules and laws, their determination is not important, their implementation is. When the worldly body of humankind, private life, emotions etc. are reflected in the management of complex interest relationships, objectivity and justice cannot be maintained in decisions. Close blame yourself, away from the criminal justice to protect, you can easily eat someone else's rights. Ultimately, when mistrust in human justice reaches a peak level, it has become inevitable that refuge is sought in digital justice and the **Digital Judge** period started.*

The Digital Judge, can be interpreted as a machine version of man with human failures and weaknesses removed. Who wants a justice system that creates doubt? When I am within the Thinkmatic, how do I have a say in the management of the Thinkmatic?

Heaven: If you look at it with simple logic, you are the one about which a decision is made, and you can affect the decisions made with the choices you make. Take a ride in the car to the city, one also secretly thought that you follow the helicopter. In this case the person in the helicopter will know what street you are travelling, at what speed, and how you are going, whether you are complying with the rules or not. Again as the person in the helicopter looks from above, they can see all the roads you can take and all the buildings you can stop off on during this route, but they cannot know which road or which building you will choose. When you suddenly turn back, left, right or stop, the helicopter will be forced to match you and do the same. To learn more about your choices according to your choices moving helicopter, you are actually managing. You are it, it is you.

"It is You, You're It" I've heard all over the world "Actually, He You, You're It" Can we open a little?

Heaven: The logic is very simple; something for you, if you are moving according to that thing, it's you, You're it!

Now let us consider that a large town as been emptied and turned into a track in order to carry out selection of the best driver, and let us give only starting and finish points.

Saving monitor without moving the candidates, evaluating the referee Suppose also that the helicopter. The referee at the beginning of the competition knows as a possibility where the contestant can go and where they can stop, but cannot know what route the contestant will take. Already contest where the contestants and the purpose is to determine how it will go. Let's consider a situation where the contestants notice the helicopter intuitively but cannot physically see it.

Candidates from the starting point of the car, after the start of the competition usually do the following selections:

1. *No racing for a while after they are drawn to the race or committed suicide.*

2. *Not receiving a very serious race walking around so idly, they live as passive competitors.*

3. *Some pull the car over and beg those in the helicopter to show them the way. They want those in the helicopter to feel sorry for them and help them. Instead of racing they try to beg and gain an advantage. Serious shows with rich content can be developed in this.*

4. *Some, in order for the helicopter to show the way and do them a favour are closing in and offering promises and vows as bribes. They try to prove themselves with their appearance and clothes.*

5. *Those who try to reach the goal by making do with what they have at hand and being thankful.*

6. *Some continue on their road and say to those in the helicopter "Give me a faster car, this car is too slow, watch me, I am ready for more serious exams! What can I do to break records?". (Level increase request)*

7. ***Those who have finished the race in a short period and have solved the system,*** *by saying, "As you can see I am passing these roads and tests with ease. I have solved the workings of the system. These races no longer give me pleasure, I want to go up in the helicopter, be one of those who determines the race courses and track, who evaluates the results", they are making a claim for the* ***technical team and want to be one of the new heirs of the system and become one of the administrators of the system.***

It works like this in the Thinkmatic, sometimes this is a challenging car race, sometimes it is the Istanbul / Nirvana road and the deadly forest, sometimes it is a marriage, sometimes a manager at a workplace, a worker, a boss, it doesn't matter. Options and election system so simple.

What I do not understand the personal benefits as a justice of the digital judges. Can we reinforce this with an example?

PERSONAL JUSTICE AND DIGITAL JUDGE

Heaven: *Personalized **"Individual and Criminal Justice System"***

Justice; provided the court is bound to judge justice. This questioning of the safest, most reliable evidence of that, and thus the court that reviews the least. The judge in the court where the information is more or less engaged in unhealthy review. Therefore, "Justice judge depends, not to judge justice."

Let's consider this example: The aim in giving 20 years imprisonment to people who have been imprisoned for murder; is to relieve the relatives of the murdered person, the person who committed the crime to understand their error and no commit a crime again upon release.

So how was determined that 20 years of life as the life of the killed against death? The aim is to bring the situation will not repeat the same offense due to human error and is to make sure that:

1. Asking regret, and one that accesses a maturity period of 2 years (20-2 = 18years) will be in vain or imprisonment. 18 years extra bed for person, other crimes can even bring jobs situation.

2. If he is a person who is to be released because he has completed the time, if he has planned new murders which he will commit as soon as he is released and he is to commit new murders, then at that time a potential criminal who should not be released will have been released early.

In the current system, unfortunately the answers to these questions are learnt only when there is a huge loss of people. It is that being unaware of true intent which has forced people into a fixed penalty system which is the most unsuccessful system and where human decisions are made independent of people in place of a customized justice system.

At the base of this penalty system, just like in feuds, there is the taking of one life for another. The only difference from a real feud, is that in place of the life of the criminal being taken straight away, it is taken over a long period in the corners of prisons. So to speak, between the state and the offender is conducting a vendetta carried out by the state.

Society, one loses one of the two people in jail grave. One has gone anyway, and if there are any we can save we must try everything for this. **"Delayed Justice is Injustice".** *Drew the penalty is injustice every day in prison for the extra one that could be useful to society.*

Who has not broken your laws, you say?
What's the taste of a sinless life, you say?
I do evil, if you paid evils,
You remain difference between what I say, you say?
Ömer HAYYAM

Basically, the information and methods from the future must not be just one that punishes people more or lowers the crime rate, it must also include methods which recover individuals who have committed crimes back into society by offering new horizons and new chances for those who repent to show their repentance.

State fair to leave need to seek justice for its citizens in all fields must establish systems. Why or punishment of the criminals in jail, is relieved and the community close to the deceased. Should the person who has committed a crime be able to sufficiently convince the relatives of the deceased, judges and the public of their repentance and that they will not commit a crime again, then the criminal can be allowed to return to their normal live, and if they can't, then this means the feud in accordance with the law continues.

As all records of the murder are recorded in the memory of the criminal, those records are taken and converted into simulation scenarios in the Thinkmatic. In order to understand whether a person will commit a crime again or not, the person will be goaded with the same feelings of hatred due to the scenarios prior to the murder without knowing why they are there, and the illusion image of the murdered person ruled by the central brain goads the murderer in the same way.

If the remorse that a person experiences is a remorse that goes down to the depths of the consciousness, that has been ingrained on the depths of the soul, the person will take notice of the don't do it warnings coming from their essence, and will despite all goading remain calm and not commit the murder.

The rule that the person who does not commit a crime in the Thinkmatic will not commit a crime in the real world is tested by goading more and more in Thinkmatic scenarios. When the Thinkmatic gives a report that this criminal will no longer commit a crime, the Thinkmatic records are shown to the judges, the family of the deceased and anyone who wishes to see them. Would be guilty of reintegration with their acquiescence. Thus, the "Technological Fairness", "Digital Justice", "Digital Judge" era began.

There was a hope for everyone to jail initially this technology. Thus by entering the brain records of the person said to be guilty, the information is obtained as to whether they committed the crime or not or under what conditions the crime was committed without any doubt, and the transition to special justice was provided for the person.

Just like my father's method of testing the apprentice, "The person tested in an uncontrolled environment, decides with his own essential self". With guides, channelled knowledge, documents etc, intuitively you have been in constant contact throughout the history with people. What changed now?

Heaven: *This information flow which we call classic information transfer methods are always continuing in all ways. We always have a one way communication network with mankind* *consisting of our recommendations through books, films, bit players etc. When the technological knowledge and experience in the Thinkmatic get very close to the level of being able to make the Thinkmatic, by opening the mystery veil between them another level we initiate the Golden Age of Knowledge and start the transition of mankind to the Divine Knowledge Dimension.*

Why Now?

Heaven: *If you notice you are not rejecting anything explained here as I do not understand, impossible, not possible etc. and you are understanding everything you have heard easily. Because with the documentary channel, technological, scientific and spiritual information you have obtained by watching them instead of soaps, magazine programs, matches etc in the world dimension, you have created the technical infrastructure for here very well. When what they know nears the system creation technology, this compulsory contact which is the detailed transition plan begins automatically. If you pay attention to the latest films, documentaries, Virtual Reality is continually and with new perspectives always on the agenda.*

Were you inspired in this amazing technology by Holy books?

Heaven: *We have divided not only the holy books, but all ancient information given to society, as based on wisdom and intuition. We called the Sociological Verses or Sociological Information, which explain subjects such as sin / good deed regarding the earth and world dimensions, God or Sociological*

God they described, the verses regarding technological subjects related to the creation and the design of the universe Technological Verses, Technological Information, and the God they described as the Technological God.

Instead of looking at miracles described in holy books or history as supernatural events for God to prove himself to people, for his prophets to be believed in, to facilitate faith and reinforce faith, we saw them as future goals given to humanity. Thus, by reaching the awareness that the explained miracle is more than what is explained, we conducted a new future modelling. The cases seen as miracles in the past and the characteristics of the prophet, such as making the blind see, the cripple walk, resurrecting the dead (under certain conditions) etc. are now partially possible by many medical people/scientists. They also like the miracle, doctors also hope the prophet. Because now turned into an ordinary event. So, it was renewed faith with science.

You wrote the Holy Technological Design and usage areas of technological verses which you learned in education in 2009 in detail in the "New Reasons to Believe" book. You will be notified of the maximum size Dreammatic in reality come out of the design and Fearmatic here. *We share an important part of the whole adventure in the light of the knowledge.*

An amazing preparatory school, I realized that everything I learned and experienced in the Thinkmatic has prepared me for an super world mission plan. How will I act towards something that knows my every move in advance, which can

rule my thoughts and feelings without my knowledge, how will I pass the tests?

Heaven: The reason for its closeness, and all life events that you have experienced, was because it was a game to try to understand you and find what is most suitable to you. Think of it as a development process where you are trying to be made to believe not through fear or incentives, but by recommendations, words, events, which persuade you and convince you.

Be brave, experience unconditional trust and surrender, don't forget that small efforts will initiate great changes in your life, and always make the effort and have the courage to be yourself.

UNCONDITIONAL TRUST AND
COMPLETE SURRENDER

In this system which does not have a beginning, "Complete Surrender" is discussed everywhere but I don't think I fully understand it.

Heaven: As a result of creation, you accept quicker that whose beginning is not known, and love more that whose end is not known. *What do you understand if I say behave as you like?*

I would behave without thinking about what others would say. I would be myself.

Heaven: *Automatic means "behavior performed out of will." The will is the "power to decide to do something or not" It is the process where you decide to do or not to do something following the reasoning consisting of worries and fears occurring, with the awareness of something coming from within or from your essence. It takes time and might lead to a fundemental change. Thinkmatic be aware that the world has no worries and fears will govern. Thinkmatic thoughts are automatic version, called so Thinkmatic. For it to become a word or an action, a physical output from your core self, just as it is an electrical or biochemical action in your brain, it can directly take this raw information and interpret it before you do. Know before you. But you can change this raw information to the world consciousness. That is when, when you feel entirely safe within yourself, when you can bypass your fears, doubts, cost, benefit filter and experience complete submission, when you can be yourself without touching the information coming from your essence, that is the moment You and You, You are Him, you are integrated and now "ONE".*

Never forget that the fundamental nature of man is cooperation, that it is not just shaping material which represents intelligence, gains or sovereignty, that they are programmed to help others, and use this outside as love, sharing and cooperation. This will make you and consistent with its nature. That the emotional crowd, everything is ready to replace it with a better you know. In this book, share with everyone, and not allow anyone to contribute. Do not be one of those who, when it ends, answers the question "What were you lacking to succeed?" with "I had nothing lacking but courage and effort!". Up till now you were a believer, now be one of those who makes you believe... You were one who awoke, now be the one who awakens... Move from individual scenarios to complete scenarios...

When matter and anti-matter, the visible and invisible parts of matter come together, they are transformed into energy and they disappear. The knowledge beyond time and space was reached, and the invisible lock of the world was unlocked. As the curtain between the visible and the invisible has been lifted, is there still a reason for me to live in a system which obtains its power from there being no resolution?

Heaven: *Does education ever end in an unlimited design? There is the next stage the GRUPMATIC but we can't talk about this now. Now as the understanding stage is ending for you, the explanation and development stage has begun. You are now in the buffer zone, you know here, and the Thinkmatic and the Dreammatic. Don't tire yourself too much trying to understand where you are. After a while in the early stages of this transition period that is based on time and space, where you doubt all acceptance of reality, you get used to it. As you said; 'It is not important to solve the system but to endure after you solve it.'*

Good luck with your first day in the new dimension. Old world and new realities. Welcome to holy solitude! When you prove your Unconditional Belief, we have brought you to conscious awareness at a point where we can see this contact will not change your belief. If your belief had become compulsory belief,

*belief becomes acceptance and you wouldn't have made the que-
ries you did today. Complete submission is not absolute obedience.*

**I am in a case where I am right on the margin, where both
sides are meaningless. Am I in the dream that God has created, or in the dream that you have created? Virtual, or real? That's the whole point! What if I cannot get used to this
unanswered and uneasy situation?**

*Heaven: Welcome to the Golden Age of Knowledge where there
is no time and space. If you cannot be sure of time and space,
the only things you are certain of will be knowledge and awareness. Don't worry, if you have been able to make it this far, of
course you will get used to it! If you cannot get used to it, the
lower level of reality will begin again, and you will keep trying
until you get used to it. It is not important in whose dream you
are living, it is to manage your own dream and see your own
dream. You are between dreams and reality, and you will never
be sure which you are in. This will motivate you, you will always
be diligent and productive. That is why we say, "Before you understand what you are in, do not decide how you will live!.*

*Consider that on a highway with a speed limit of 130 km, there
are speed radar cameras every ten kilometres. You will whether
you wish to or not slow down at each one, maybe you will then
accelerate, but you will not know whether the camera is working
or not without passing it at excessive speed. When the fine arrives at home, you will be more careful on your next trip and*

you will not speed. When the fine does not arrive you will say it doesn't work anyway and you will speed without worry. If you get a fine this time, you will be constantly diligent because you do not know whether it works or not.

When a girlfriend said about a multi floor lighting shop they were going to open that "I don't know how we will ever prevent theft with a few personnel"; I said, "I think you should write all over the store "THIS STORE IS PROTECTED BY HIDDEN SECURITY CAMERAS". Thieves who see the writing and believe there are hidden cameras will give up on it. Even the possibility will be a deterrent.

Heaven: The possibility of an observer is very effective on the movements of the observed. In this dimension, the selection of politicians is not carried out with public elections but by the Thinkmatic. Those who wish to take the position of Prime Minister, MP etc, will be subject to each scenario such as, will they give favours to Party members, family members, friends etc. in tenders, land, cadastre etc.? Will they abuse their position? Does he have the interests of the country and the nation? Are they brave? They will be tested according to all scenarios with the Thinkmatic. The people will not choose anyone. The candidates will prove themselves in a virtual environment in political scenarios. The administration will be given to the one with the highest breaking point.

Even if you have difficulties in this intellectual transition it is very colourful to live in the middle. You can be on whatever side you want, when you want. When you are bored of one, who wouldn't want the other?

While you are transitioning from one to the other, you are distancing yourself from one and not yet reaching the other and you do not belong to either side entirely. What is difficult in this intellectual transition, is the possibility of both sides being illusion and reality, and never being sure. The stage where secrets are not safe, where you can never be sure of who is who, where there is even the possibility that material is not real, where the worldly pleasures and material greed of man ends.

Heaven: *Old ideas are so ingrained that as a new answer is an unacceptable reality, even those who find it can doubt their answers. At this stage where time and space lose their meaning, the only thing to take you out of this mental prison, is knowledge and awareness. You must say "God Increase My Knowledge". When you are suffering, remember the Spiritual power within you. (We had come to an experience I had had in 1994)*

In 1994, I was home alone one night on one of the days where everything was going wrong and I had lost nearly everything spiritually and financially. Suddenly I started to become agitated, I started to perceive and see the world abnormally, I started to experience a problem of just not fitting in. I was in trouble where talking to someone, going out etc. or in other worlds humanity and the world just wasn't enough, and which was constantly increasing.

While I was losing control of my senses and body due to this issue which I could not define, I started to say "I will soon go crazy". Just at this point where what is visible is not enough, I remembered the angels that were placed in my command at the first Creation by God and which would be responsible for me. Two or three minutes after I said " I call all angels/guides at my service to come here and help me. "Come immediately and help me" I slept in peace. Thus, I learnt that prayer cannot just be in the format of a desire but as a command too.

Heaven: Desire and emotional disruption force a person to think and ensure his awareness or awakening. For someone to realize the power that they have, sometimes we have to make things very difficult, and bring them to the point that they have nothing to lose.

At first when you said "Make a wish to US, whatever it is. Say LET THERE BE so it is right away", what would have happened if I had said nothing?

Heaven: We offer but we do not insist. You would continue with your sleep, and would have woken up to a new day at your life in the Thinkmatic. But not everything can be determined with a single question. The processes you experience determine the questions to be asked of you.

THE THEORY OF EVERYTHING = THE THEORY OF EVERYONE

It is a theory that explains the universe. A theory that explains how the universe works and the reason behind it... A unifying theory. Stephen Hawking said in **his** book A Brief History of Time, page 185: *"If we do discover a complete theory, it should in time be understandable in broad principle by everyone, not just a few scientists. Then shall all philosophers, scientists, and just ordinary people, be able to take part in the discussion of the question of the universe and how we exist. If we find the answer to that, it would be the ultimate triumph of human reason for then we would know the mind of God."*

With these words, as an ordinary human being, I thought that science should give me courage. ***"A theory that a person on the street is able to understand and discuss is a theory they can discover. Therefore I said: "The Theory of Everything = Everyone's Theory."***

Since the question is asked so that everyone can understand it, the answer should be in a form everyone can reach. If the answer to God was hidden in a form only scientists or religious men could find, then it would be unfair to ordi-

nary people. As it is, to show the simplicity of the hidden answer, prophets were chosen from ordinary people.
"The Theory of Everything = Everyone's Theory."

No Black Holes Exist, Says Stephen Hawking—At Least Not Like We Think
http://news.nationalgeographic.com/news/2014/01/140127-black-hole-stephen-hawking-firewall-space-astronomy/

'The conventional view of black holes posits that their gravitational pull is so powerful that nothing can escape from them—not even light, which is why they're called black holes. The boundary past which there is supposedly no return is known as the event horizon. In this conception, all information about anything that ventures past a black hole's event horizon is destroyed. On the other hand, quantum physics, the best description so far of how the universe behaves on a subatomic level, suggests that information cannot ever be destroyed, leading to a fundamental conflict in theory.

Now Hawking is suggesting a resolution to the paradox: Black holes do not possess event horizons after all, so they do not destroy information.'

What Hawking was saying briefly in a paper he posted on-line on January 22 was 'Knowledge remains where matter is gone'.

What I say is that 'Everything' consists of time and space. When you understand that you are in a dream, the time and space you live in lose their meaning. You cannot bring in anything to a dream or cannot take away anything from a dream. Just like you cannot bring in anything to this world or cannot take away anything from this world when you are leaving it. The only thing that remains is the KNOWLEDGE. Time and space exist for the purpose of Knowledge and they only consist of knowledge. If we say,

M=Matter, t=Time, ◎ = Knowledge,

We Can Say

M + t = ◎ for the Theory of Everything.

AFTERWORD & INVITATION

The personal successes and failures as well as the happiness and the unhappiness that we experienced have helped us specialize in different areas of the whole. Calm down, you are specializing in subjects that you are experiencing with your concealed memory of the past in a Thinkmatic scenario that was totally your choice. Work and show your effort relentlessly.

You have learnt the fundamental principles of the Age of Golden Age where everything is designed and discovered from the beginning and even the minor things can create a crucial awareness. While reckoning what hasn't been conceived yet, let us be amongst those who write about, explain and design the future. Let us be one of those who think and make others think.

Let us receive the Nobel Peace prize all together with our book which aims to maintain peace with everything.

If you knew that you were to complete in an illusionary track which was designed for you to specify your breaking points and talents, and knew that it would get ever more difficult in time, would you choose the easiest or the hardest one when you are selecting the starting criterion? Please fill out the Thinkmatic Application Form thinking about this choice and sign it. Live your life thinking about it for a while.

I am ever ready to change my knowledge and experiences that I present to you, with more advanced ones.

Wishing that you live your life thinking and making others think...

May you be enlightened and enlighten others...

Aydın TÜRKGÜCÜ
aturkgucu@gmail.com   www.aydinturkgucu.net

APPLICATION FOR THINKMATIC

(The less the chances there are, the more the points you have)

SUBJECT	VALUE
Subject factor Which subject do you wish to test: Profession, heroism, administration, talents, justice, marriage, courage, a combination of these or all?	--
Period Factor Higher points for promises quickly kept	1/life
Term Beginning Factor The later the date the higher the possibilities and education. Higher points for fewer possibilities	1/birth year
Financial/psychological support from family factor Higher points for persons closer and fewer for family that understand and support you. Mother/father=3, Sibling=2, other relative=1	1/person x value + 1/person x value +...
Financial/psychological support from others factor Higher points for lower number of persons who understand or support you. i.e. You choose a person from your family to help. Since it is family, you get fewer points. When you choose someone from your outer circle of friends, since you have to contact that person somehow to get help, you get extra points for the trouble. *Close=1, Unknown=2, Enemies=3 (gaining the respect of your enemies gains you higher points)*	1/person x value + 1/person x value +....
Financial/psychological help from your work place Factor The life course is above all a fight to stay alive. Therefore, help from your work friends is very important.	1/person

Health factor or physical capability factor (HF) This reminds me of people at the beach who claim they can swim well; when someone claims he could swim a certain distance with one arm, for example. Anything that would hinder will increase points. For those who feel that if they have a certain illness they will finish sooner; Asthma/rheumatic fever=4, heart=5, partial blindness=6, hand/foot=7, ALS =10	Health factor 1 + Health factor 2 + Health factor 3...
Education level factor Reducing: Whatever education level you mark that is below standard levels will be an extra point. Increasing: the upper level you can attain is measured. Any level you attain above the level you chose will give you an extra point.	1/level Level 1+level 2 +.....
Spouse by your side factor On the racecourse of life, a spouse is a great help to the soul. The longer you can delay marking this field, the more points you will have. I wonder if those who never marry did not check this factor.	Marriage year
Number of problem children factor When children become caring adults, they can make life easier; if in childhood or adulthood, they are ill or somehow abnormal they can make life difficult. In this case, the abnormal child can add points.	Number of abnormal children
Difficult Environment Think of the things you have succeeded doing in your life; if you had a chance to repeat them would you be able to do them is such difficult, Justice, War, Global warming, environments? Economic crisis	Sum of the fields of difficulty
Economic Situation Factor Think of this as the initial investment. There is a difference in suc-	1/beginning in-

ceeding from poverty and from wealth. Each situation has its pluses and minuses. But money is a serious support. So the less the initial investment, the more points gained. The important thing here is not where you began, but what you contributed.	vestment
Country Factor What country will you be doing what you intended to do: England, USA, Germany, Turkey, Iraq, China, Russia, the Far East, African countries etc. Each one has plus or minus points according to the situations surrounding your subject in that country in the period you live there: more difficult = more points.	1/country
General TOTAL	
Name, Surname	**Signature**

RESOURCES

Aydın TÜRKGÜCÜ, 1996, İsimsiz Kitap, Ankara

Aydın TÜRKGÜCÜ, 1998, Ben Hazırım Başlasın, Ankara, Exit

Aydın TÜRKGÜCÜ, 2006, Konsantre Kur'an-ı Kerim, Ankara, Exit

Aydın TÜRKGÜCÜ, 2007, Sanal tanrı, Ankara, Exit

Aydın TÜRKGÜCÜ, 2009, İnanmak İçin Yeni Sebepler, Ankara, Exit

Beyza BİLGİN Prof.Dr., 2005, İslamda Kadının Rolü Türkiye'de Kadın, Ankara, Sinemis

Burhan YILMAZ, 2005, Bilinmeyen Mevlana, İstanbul, Kozmik Kitaplar

Ergun CANDAN, 1998, Gizli Sırlar Öğretisi, İstanbul, Sınır Ötesi Yayıncılık

Fatma PAKSÜT Dr., 1980, Platon ve Platon Sonrası, Ankara.

Dr. Bedri RUHSELMAN, İlahi Nizam ve Kainat, İstanbul, Ruh ve Madde

Jeanette EATON, 1961, Gandhi, Kılıçsız Mücahid, İst., Amerikan Bord Neşriyat D..

John BROCKMAN, 2002, The Next Fifty Years, NewYork, Vintage

Karen ARMSTRONG, 2007, Tanrının Tarihi, Ankara, Ayraç

Kenan GÜRSOY, Prof. Dr., 2007, Maurice Merleau-Ponty'de Algı Prob. Giriş, Lotus.

Kitabı Mukaddes, 1995, Eski ve Yeni Ahit, Kitabı Mukaddes Şirketi

Martin LİNGS (Ebubekir Siraceddin), 2006, Hz. Muhammed'in Hayatı, İst. İnsan Yay.

Orhan HANÇERLİOĞLU, 2008, Düşünce Tarihi, İstanbul, Remzi Kitabevi

Oruç ARUOBA (Türkçesi), Deccal, Hil Yayınevi

Osman KARABULUT, 1994, Şems-i TEBRİZİ - Mevlana, Konya, Şems Yayınları

Sinan CANAN Dr., 2008, Fraktal Düşünceler, Ankara, Haber/Ajanda

Stephen W. HAWKING / Leonard Mlodinow, 2005, A Briefer History Of Time, Banta

Stephen W. HAWKİNG, 1988, A Brief History Of Time, U.K., Bantam

Stephen W. HAWKİNG, 1994, Black Holes And Baby Universes, U.K., Bantam

Stephen W. HAWKİNG, Stephen Hawking'le Zaman ve Uzayda Gezinti, İstanbul, Alkım

Turgut ÖZGÜNEY, Pythagoras, İstanbul

Dogukan Murathan YÜCEL http://www.dmy.info/

Kozan DEMİRCAN http://khosann.com

www.mysubh.com

SEMINARS

Anadolu Aydınlanma Vakfı (2014), Araştırmalar Enstitüsü, Aşkın Özüne Dönüş, Bilgi Paylaşım, Brahma Kumaris (2014), Holistik Akademi (2013-2014), Kabuljan Murzaev ve Mahram Satymbaeva (2014), Naturel Fuarı (2013-2014), Nişdo-Rgm

Ali Seydi GÜLTEKİN (Dr.) & Servet GÜLTEKİN, Aydın ARITAN, Belma YENER (Dr.), Bihin EDİGE, Bora TURGAY, Canan YOLAÇ, Cavit UTKU, Deniz Şifa OFLAZ, Ebru ATALAY, Ergun ARIKDAL, Evren GÖNENÇ (Dr.), farah YURDÖZÜ, Füsun Çil TAŞLI, Haluk Berkmen (Dç.Dr.), Hande AKIN, Hülya KAVUZLU, Hüseyin UYSAL (Prof.Dr.), Işık YAZAN, Metin BOBAROĞLU, Murat KIRHAN, Oğuzhan AKOVA, Orhan KURAL (Prof.Dr.), Özcan KÖKNEL (Prof.Dr.), Özün KANBAY, Salih AKDEMİR (Prof.Dr.), Serpil Kuruşkanat DAĞLI, Şevki CAN & Belir Yöney CAN, Şule KOCADÖLÜ, Tarık ARIKDAL, Ulviye DOĞAN, Ülkü KALMAZ, Ümit ORMAN, Yurdaay ONARAN, Yusuf Kenan ARATAN

(Alfabetic order.)

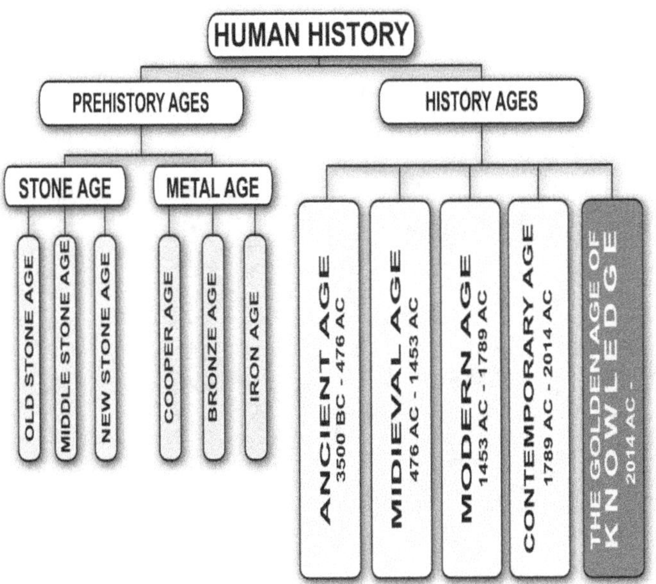

The human history have been divided into ages according to the tools that were used and the important social and political events that had an effect on human history. Now for the first time in history, it is named according to the time and space that's lived in.

Aydın TÜRKGÜCÜ
Thinker & Thought-Stimulator

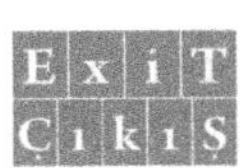

ISBN 978-975-6861-06-6

9 789756 861066